*Materials and Their Applications
in Landscape Design*

Materials and Their Applications in Landscape Design

Rob W. Sovinski, ASLA

John Wiley & Sons, Inc.

Images courtesy of Eric Anderson Productions: Figure 7.5; Figure 7.8; Figure 9.4; Pavements I colorplate, bottom left image; Pavements II colorplate, top right image; Pavements III colorplate, top left image; Walls II colorplate; top left image

Images courtesy of Sundown Gardens. Figure 8.1

For general information about our other products and services, please contact our Customer Care Department within the United States at (800) 762-2974, outside the United States at (317) 572-3993 or fax (317) 572-4002.

Wiley also publishes its books in a variety of electronic formats. Some content that appears in print may not be available in electronic books. For more information about Wiley products, visit our web site at www.wiley.com.

Library of Congress Cataloging-in-Publication Data:

Sovinski, Rob W.
    Materials and their applications in landscape design / Rob Sovinski.
        p.   cm.
Includes bibliographical references and index.
    ISBN 978-0-470-11293-9 (cloth/website)
        1. Landscape construction—Materials.   2. Building materials.   3. Landscape design.   I. Title.
TH4961.S68   2009
624—dc22
                                                                2008019007

Printed in the United States of America

10 9 8 7 6 5 4 3 2 1

*For Margot, Robin, Teddy, and Jane,
and with great appreciation to my mentors
in landscape architecture, Ted Walker,
Carl Steinitz, and Campbell Miller*

CONTENTS

PREFACE

Before human intervention and modification, nature provided the earth with a landscape. It was a landscape that was characterized by contradiction. It was subject to frequent, often cataclysmic change and yet functioned in idyllic, Eden-like harmony. For most of the creatures on the planet, it was a landscape without any particular need for improvement. For humans, the experience of the natural landscape was different. For the overwhelming majority of human history, the unaltered landscape represented a hostile and threatening wilderness, one whose destiny was alteration at the hands of humans.

The historical record suggests that among our many activities, we humans are, at our core, changers of the landscape . . . unabashed tinkerers who cannot leave well enough alone. For a myriad of reasons that have been well documented, and some that we still do not fully understand, we are compelled to alter

Whether by design or the spontaneous whimsy of a worker, this rosette is a delightful discovery in an otherwise undifferentiated field of stone paving.

Though utterly natural in feel, the hand of a skilled designer is clearly evident in these compelling stone steps.

the wafer-thin surface stratum of our planet that we inhabit, its *landscape*. We pave for commerce and trade; we wall for security and containment; we build for shelter and comfort. But we also landscape for delight, for food, for cultural expression, and even for spirituality. The sum of our landscape-changing activity suggests not so much that we are not well suited to live in the original landscape offered up by nature, but rather that we possess a fundamental need—even obsession—to reconfigure the world we inhabit.

Even as we alter nature, the materials of our revised landscapes are, for the most part, taken from nature. Stone and brick; wood and aggregate; iron and water: These are the basic building blocks of Japanese gardens, Italian piazzas, English parks, and the American corporate campus. Our insatiable appetite to alter the landscape again and again hints that nature is somehow inadequate, not up to the task. Suggesting that we can do better than nature even smacks of arrogance, yet we honor that same nature as we celebrate the beauty and utility of its raw materials, which form the basis of our landscape palette.

Within each material there resides a dual nature that designers have an obligation to understand and respect. Each material must be used in a manner compatible with its engineering, structural, and technical characteristics. If we fail to understand the limits and capabilities of materials, we condemn our projects to certain failure and its users to inconvenience or even hazard. Each material must also be understood in terms of its aesthetic, right-brained possibilities. If we fail to tap into the spirit and beauty inherent in materials, our projects have no rightful place in the human theater. Vitruvius, the first century B.C. Roman architect, suggested that all human construction carries the burden of three primary objectives: *firmitas, utilitas,* and *venustas.* These continue to serve as trustworthy benchmarks. Despite ever-changing styles and paradigms, ensuring that the built environment is durable, that it is useful, and that it delights and enriches us carries as much significance now as in ancient Rome.

Those individuals engaged in landscape architecture and landscape design often engage a long-running debate that seeks to define landscape design alternatively as a pursuit that is primarily engineering oriented and problem-solving, or as an artistic, creative outlet for the avant garde. The answer to this debate is "yes." The best landscape designers draw from a keen technical expertise combined with unbridled artistic creativity in the pursuit of meaningful and lasting solutions.

It follows that any text dealing with the building blocks of the landscape must also be about *firmitas, utilitas,* and *venustas.* It must be equal parts right-brained and left-brained. It is impossible to instruct students in the technical characteristics of materials without also addressing their inherent aesthetic characteristics: not in a separate course nor in a parallel studio, but at the same moment within the same design challenge. Every creative design inspiration becomes reality only via an appropriate technical solution, just as every technical configuration carries with it a unique opportunity to express the artistic human urge. How we build informs what we build exactly as what we build informs how we build.

ACKNOWLEDGMENTS

I would like to express my gratitude to the following:

Brenda Beitler Bowen, PhD, Assistant Professor of Geology, Purdue University, for assisting with the chapter *Geology 101*

Eric Anderson, Eric Anderson Productions, for taking time during his Italian excursion to photograph landscape details instead of monuments

Jay Rients, Commercial Design Consultant, Unilock Chicago, Inc., for his contribution of time and expertise to this undertaking, and to the education of Purdue Landscape Architecture students

Brian Trimble, Brick Industry Association, Director of Engineering Services and Architectural Outreach, for his substantial contributions to my first book, *Brick in the Landscape*, from which much of the brick-related material in this book was drawn

A NOTE TO INSTRUCTORS

Landscape designers are fortunate people. We work with materials that are rich and organic: stone, wood, earth, iron, copper. These are highly rewarding materials steeped in timeless tradition and enhanced over time with the warmth of patina. They are also demanding materials. To capture the soul of a stone requires a deep respect for the millions of years it took nature to give it form. Granite speaks to the formation of the earth itself. To work with brick requires knowledge of its rich traditions and history of craftsmanship. To detail with wood demands that we understand the very cell structure of the living tree from which the lumber was milled.

A key issue in the preparation of this text was what to include and what to leave out. It is a simple notion to suggest that we need to teach design students to *design*, not to *build*. Designers work at drawing tables and computers, not in a stone quarry or a lumber mill. They need to know enough about materials to use them intelligently and aesthetically, but they do not need to learn how to lay brick or to pour concrete. That is true enough. Given the years of training and apprenticeship required of a bricklayer, or a stonemason, it would be sheer arrogance to suggest that designers could even approach their skill and knowledge. Nevertheless, *some* knowledge of production and of the jobsite is critical for designers. If the masonry cavity wall detail we draw does not call for adequate clear space between the brick and the concrete masonry backup, the bricklayer's knuckles will be bruised and tender by the end of the day and the internal drainage of that wall will be impeded by the mortar droppings trapped in the undersized cavity. If we never observe a stone-cutting saw in action, it is unlikely that we will understand the issues related to countless complex cuts and the unnecessary waste of costly material.

Manufacturing, quarrying, or harvesting the raw materials for the built landscape is not the task of the designer—but those operations each exert their unique own set of effects on the cost, sustainability, social equity, and *genius loci* of a material and site. What are the opportunities to reclaim an exhausted stone aggregate quarry? How has the chemistry of pressure-treating wood changed in the past twenty-five years? Which common landscape material is petroleum-based and carries some of the political and economic baggage of that particular resource?

This text is written to introduce students and self-learners to a broad range of traditional and emerging materials and their uses in landscape design. It is organized and edited to provide an overview that touches on the design, economic, environmental, functional, and practical issues of material selection, layout, and detailing. Landscape designers need to make thoughtful, informed decisions regarding the built landscape. A text that aspires to address such a broad spectrum of materials could easily grow to be an unwieldy tome. That would not be a helpful tool in the education of landscape designers. What is needed is a carefully struck balance between breadth and depth. That was the single-minded goal of this text.

Thoughtful, intelligent design transcends catalogue cuts and sample boards. It entails a fundamental knowledge of acquisition, manufacturing, implementation, and life-cycle performance of the materials that occupy the designer's palette. Material choices, detailing, configuration, and layout have far-reaching impacts on quality of life. Thoughtless design may be oblivious to that responsibility but affects those realms nonetheless.

Materials and Their Applications in Landscape Design cannot stand alone in the education and training of anyone pursuing a career in landscape design or landscape architecture. It is intended to work in concert with a broad curriculum in design practice and theory, plant materials, professional practice, natural land systems, and human interventions. This text aspires to serve as a key contributing resource in the education and training of complete landscape designers.

Materials and Their Applications in Landscape Design

MATERIALS AND SUSTAINABILITY

SUSTAINABILITY FACTORS

Determining the overall sustainability of a potential construction material is surprisingly complex. Materials that perform well after installation may require tremendous amounts of energy to manufacture or may involve environmentally hazardous methods to acquire. The impacts associated with materials prior to installation may be less visible to the user but are nonetheless critical factors in measuring a material's overall sustainability. For every material, there are six distinct stages during which its sustainability can be measured.

1. *Acquisition.* Stone is quarried and wood is harvested. The raw materials for metal are mined. The clay for bricks comes from the soil itself. Each procedure requires the expenditure of energy and each impacts the pre-existing natural landscape to some degree. Responsible acquisition means finding ways to acquire materials while minimizing the associated impacts.

2. *Manufacture or Fabrication.* This step includes activities like the milling of lumber, the firing of bricks, and the forging of cast iron. It always requires energy that may or may not be readily apparent. We know that brick requires kilns heated to temperatures to achieve the necessary vitrification for production. It may be less obvious that Portland cement also requires high temperatures for its production. No material reaches its construction-ready condition without the consumption of energy.

3. *Transport.* Construction materials tend to be heavy. Bricks, stone, concrete, and wood require heavy machinery and large vehicles to reach the job site. Selecting granite from overseas requires a significantly higher amount of energy than

domestic stone. This impact is significant, and LEED (Leadership in Energy and Environmental Design) awards points to projects whose materials were delivered within a close proximity to the jobsite.

4. *Installation.* Site preparation typically requires the displacement of topsoil and the grubbing and clearing of vegetation. Soil erosion, topsoil loss, and the sedimentation of water courses need to be carefully managed during the construction phase of a project, which may last several months. The installation of landscape materials requires labor, energy, and heavy equipment. Many contractors are developing and using new tools to make installation more efficient and economical.

   Installation may also generate health hazards for workers. Crystalline silica may become airborne when bricks are cut without controlling the resulting dust. OSHA, the Occupational Safety and Health Administration, has categorized crystalline silica as a human lung carcinogen, which can lead to silicosis.

5. *In-Place Performance.* This is the most visible phase of a material's life cycle. All materials carry a measurable degree of solar reflectivity, which can impact the local microclimate. Many materials emit significant amounts of volatile organic compounds. Life span is another critical measure of a material's sustainability. A material with a relatively short life span that requires replacement initiates a new cycle of acquisition, manufacture, transport, and installation.

Drainage and water quality are also factors for assessing in-place performance, particularly for pavements. Porous asphalt is a far more effective material for controlling runoff, recharging the groundwater, and filtering certain contaminants than impervious pavement.

All materials require varying levels of maintenance during their life span. Asphalt pavements need resurfacing. Brick requires repointing. Wood must be treated with water-repelling sealants on a routine basis. These measures consume energy and may impact the performance of a material. Some of the products used for maintenance may also emit volatile organic compounds themselves or have the capacity to contaminate the soil.

6. *Demolition or Removal.* Even the most durable material will eventually reach the end of its useful life and will require removal. The most significant aspect of demolition is the recyclability of the material. Virtually all removed asphalt can be recycled into new asphalt. Concrete, metal, and wood can all be recycled into useful construction material. It is imperative that discarded construction material not end its life in a landfill.

The removal of heavy construction materials, like slabs of concrete or large areas of asphalt pavement, requires heavy equipment and significant amounts of energy, as do the procedures needed to recycle them into a usable state. Finally, the demolished material requires yet more transport to another jobsite, recycling facility, or storage area.

Making responsible choices in material selection is not one-dimensional. Specifying a material initiates a significant expenditure of energy and creates the potential for environmental harm. Designers need to consider the entire process necessary to achieve the finished project. Thanks to a growing concern of sustainable building practices, we have access to improving metrics for understanding the ramifications of our choices.

LEED

LEED is an increasingly familiar acronym among landscape design professionals. LEED stands for *Leadership in Energy and Environmental Design.* LEED was developed by the United States Green Building Council (USGBC) as a means of assessing the environmental performance of design and construction. The LEED approach has been widely embraced and has become a recognized leader in establishing performance standards for environmental design. LEED functions by assigning points for environmentally sound materials and methods.

The USGBC defines LEED as follows:

The nationally accepted benchmark for the design, construction, and operation of high performance green buildings. LEED gives building owners and operators the tools they need to have an immediate and measurable impact on their buildings' performance. LEED promotes a whole-building approach to sustainability by recognizing performance in five key areas of human and environmental health: sustainable site development, water savings, energy efficiency, materials selection, and indoor environmental quality.

Selecting and designing with hardscape materials in exterior landscape applications touches on the first four of these five areas. Landscape professionals involved with interior plantings and gardens can have a significant impact on the fifth, "indoor environmental quality."

The USGBC offers training and education to design professionals who are interested in gaining expertise in environmental design. Interested candidates may undertake training and education leading to professional accreditation known as LEEDAP. Accreditation, which is achieved via a testing process, assures clients that the decisions and proposals of accredited professionals involved in landscape architecture and design will evolve using the latest environmental standards and recommendations.

GENERAL

Stone aggregates serve a wide variety of purposes in the built landscape. Sometimes they are visible as a finish material; at other times they play a less visible supporting role. Aggregates are available in a vast range of colors and sizes for use as mulch or a top dressing. As a support material, they mitigate the movement caused by freeze and thaw cycles, provide stability, and facilitate critical drainage beneath other pavements. Aggregates are often used as a ground cover in place of vegetation where heavy water drainage and flow are likely to result in erosion. Furthermore, they do all of this at a very economic cost compared to other durable materials. People spend a great deal of their lives traveling, parking, or just relaxing on paved surfaces. Rarely do we see the tons of aggregate just beneath the surfaces that support our countless acres of pavement, nor do we fully appreciate that a significant proportion of that same asphalt and concrete is itself

Figure 1-1 *Sorted by color and graded by size, stone aggregates offer a wide range of design options*

Figure 1-2 *This aggregate installation serves as an economical, low-maintenance solution for good drainage along the foundation wall of a building.*

composed of aggregates. Exposed aggregate concrete lets the selected aggregates shine in the spotlight. More often, though, aggregates are an unseen but key constituent of concrete pavements or walls.

Like many landscape construction materials, aggregates are essentially a gift of nature that people have learned to exploit. Some aggregates were deposited by nature, the result of geologic activity such as glaciation or fluvial activity. Other aggregates are crushed by machinery from larger stones into desired size ranges. Unlike the stone we use in walls, steps, and pavements, aggregates were originally randomly deposited, and so they are typically a mix of many stone types rather than a specific single stone, such as granite or limestone.

The construction industry creates an enormous demand for aggregate materials. They serve as key components in:

Pavement base courses
Concrete mixes, both vertical and horizontal
Bituminous mixes
Pervious surface pavements

Landscape mulch and bed dressing
Drainage courses
Construction backfill

CHARACTERISTICS OF AGGREGATE

Aggregates are as hard as stone because they *are* stone. When used in concrete or asphalt pavements, they bring the strength of stone to those composite materials. When concrete or asphalt fails, it is almost never the mineral aggregate components that fail but, rather, the cementitious material that bonds them together. If an asphalt pavement were to be left unattended for several hundred years, all that would remain would be a layer of loose aggregate material.

Aggregates are often specified to be sorted by size, in a process called *grading*. A well-graded aggregate contains individual stones within a specific size range. An ungraded aggregate contains a broader range of sizes. A well-graded aggregate provides better drainage, whereas the *fines* (extremely small particles of aggregate) present in an ungraded aggregate fill

Figure 1-3 *Serving as a mulch, this well-graded aggregate bed yields effective weed and moisture control.*

a higher percentage of the voids, impeding internal drainage. A completely ungraded aggregate mix may be nearly as impervious as concrete, but it may also provide a much more stable walking or driving surface than a well-graded mix.

Figure 1-4 A well-compacted ungraded aggregate surface provides a stable and visually appealing walking surface at a far lower cost than concrete, asphalt, or masonry unit pavers.

Figure 1-5 Adequate leveling and compaction are critical when aggregate is used as a base course supporting other paving materials.

Typically, a flexible pavement calls for two subcourses of different aggregates. A graded course of gravel or crushed stone, provided for stability and drainage, may be topped with a finer course like sand to serve as a leveling or setting bed for unit pavers.

It is important to use filter fabric in this situation to facilitate drainage while preventing the finer sand from infiltrating and clogging the voids in the drainage course below.

Even though aggregates are stone, they do not require skilled masons for installation. This enhances their overall economy. This does not mean, however, that no special skills or care are required to install aggregates. It is important for installers to accurately level and compact all specified aggregate courses. Also, when aggregates are used in visual applications, the designer must carefully select their color and grain to complement the overall design palette of a specific project.

Although aggregates offer many advantages at an economic price, designers must take certain concerns into account. Gravel and crushed-stone pavements are easily displaced and require ongoing upkeep. They also make snow removal more difficult than more rigid materials, such as concrete or asphalt. Some aggregate surfaces will not adequately support canes, walkers, or wheelchairs and thus do not meet the requirements of the Americans with Disabilities Act (ADA). Also of concern are narrow-heeled shoes and outdoor furniture with thin support legs.

STANDARDS

A variety of aggregate types are commonly used in the built environment. Perhaps more than any other material, aggregates are known by local designations

Figure 1-6 *This aggregate walkway endures intense urban foot traffic while providing adequate support for the narrow legs of the site furnishings.*

that may vary from region to region. Take care to learn the local designations for aggregates wherever you undertake projects. Still, there are some more-or-less universal designations for aggregates.

Sand is a very fine aggregate material composed of silica. It is commonly used in concrete mixes, in bituminous mixes, as a setting bed for unit pavers, and in mortar mixes. Joint sand may be swept into the joints of a flexible pavement system to add stability without sacrificing drainage.

Sand is not a good choice for walkways, driveways, or mulch. It is easily displaced by traffic, wind, and weather; it clings to shoes and tires; and it is extremely popular with neighborhood cats. Beach sand is not suitable for landscape construction, for a variety of reasons. It is often too weathered and rounded from the action of the surf, and it may contain salts that can degrade masonry. Furthermore, the mining of beach sand is not a sound environmental practice. Specifications for sand typically call for ASTM C-33: *Concrete and Bedding Sand*, or ASTM C-144: *Joint Sand* (finer, for pavers) **Torpedo sand** is well suited to many landscape applications. It is a mix of sand plus fine aggregates, with nothing larger than 3/8 inches. It satisfies the criteria set forth in ASTM C-33.

Gravel is a granular aggregate material that may be composed of almost any type of rock or stone. It is usually between 2½ inches and ⅛ inches in size. It may be rounded, if it derives from a marine or fluvial source, or angular if it is a quarried and crushed product.

Bank-run gravel is deposited by nature and is weathered into smooth, rounded shapes. Because of its rounded form, it is less likely to interlock into a stable base course. Nevertheless, this same smoothed surface can be visually appealing, making it suitable for mulches, exposed-aggregate concrete, and other visible applications.

Pea gravel is a specifically graded size range of bank-run gravel. As its name suggests, it is relatively small grained, approximating the size of peas.

Crushed stone is also known as crusher-run stone. Just as its name suggests, crushed stone is produced by mechanically crushing larger stone. Its sharp, angular facets cause it to interlock and give it more stability than bank-run gravel. It is a popular material as a paving base course and is also used for gravel roads and drives, either where impervious pavement is too costly or a more drainage-friendly paving option is desired. Crushed stone is equally useful in concrete and bituminous recipes.

Designers are well advised to acquire and become familiar with their state Department of Transportation standard roadbed specifications for any project that involves roadways or parking. These stone aggregate specifications have evolved over a lengthy period of time and have been tested in countless miles of roads and highways.

SIZE AND APPLICATIONS

When a specifically graded size range of aggregate mix is required, project specifications must leave little margin for error yet they must also provide for

Sieve Size	% Passing by Weight
2"	100 (*nothing can be >2"*)
¾"	70–100 (*at least 70% must be <¾", all of it could be <¾"*)
No. 4	30–80 (*at least 30% must be <¼", but no more than 80% can be <¼"*)
No. 50	10–35 (*at least 10% must be <1/50", but no more than 35% can be <1/50"*)
No. 200	0–5 (*no fines are desired, but up to 5% of the total weight is permitted to be fine material*)

a practical range of variation. The example in the opposite column shows how aggregate size is specified, in this case for use as a paving base course. Note that the size is determined by passing the aggregate mix through a series of decreasing sieve sizes.

AGGREGATES AND THE ENVIRONMENT

Sustainable practices increasingly demand that attention be paid to water quality, drainage, and runoff. Aggregates are by nature well-draining materials that facilitate stormwater drainage and percolation into the groundwater, while serving to filter out contaminants. Pervious pavements, as opposed to porous pavements, are essentially impervious materials with voids provided in the surface area to accommodate drainage. To function, the voids must be filled with a granular aggregate material that is carefully formulated to facilitate drainage while providing a safe walking and driving surface for people of all abilities. Even so, all aggregate mixes are prone to accumulate fines and debris over time, resulting in a measurable loss of permeability.

Because stone aggregates are quarried rather than manufactured, they do not require the extremely high temperatures associated with the firing of bricks or the production of Portland cement. Production of crusher-run stone does require heavy machinery, and thus the burning of fossil fuels, but it should be noted that the source stone for crusher-run material is often the byproduct of, or waste from, larger stone quarrying and cutting operations. Thus, the crushing operation can be viewed as recycling this waste into useful construction material. The acquisition of gravel from quarries carries with it some of the same impacts associated with any quarrying or mining activity and calls for thoughtful reclamation of exhausted sites. Lastly, although aggregate is a relatively heavy material to handle and transport, it is regionally available in almost any area and thus reduces transportation cost and fuel use.

The large range of colors offered by aggregates makes satisfying solar reflectance imminently possible. Aggregates are virtually indestructible and offer an extremely long, in-place life cycle. They can also be recycled repeatedly into new applications without any measurable loss of strength or performance.

LEARNING ACTIVITIES

1. Locate the Website for your state's Highway Department or Department of Transportation.
   a. Find and print the standard specification for aggregate roadbeds.
   b. Prepare a brief summary of this specification.
2. Locate and describe examples in your area where aggregates are used for:
   a. Exposed aggregate cast-in-place concrete surfaces
   b. Mulch or top dressing
   c. Erosion control and drainage courses

CHAPTER 2 ASPHALT (BITUMINOUS CONCRETE)

GENERAL

Asphalt, also known as *bituminous concrete*, is employed in greater surface acreage than any other exterior construction material. Asphalt is economical, durable, and relatively easy to maintain and repair. Surface courses can be replaced without removing or replacing the supporting bases. Asphalt is used in site planning for parking, roads, and driveways, as well as trails, paths, and recreational courts. It is also used (to a much lesser degree) for curbing.

The first asphalt pavements in the United States, installed in the late nineteenth century, used naturally occurring lake asphalt. With the advent of the automobile, the rapid increase in the demand for smooth, paved roads quickly outpaced naturally occurring sources of asphalt. Petroleum-based asphalt was developed to meet the spiraling demand and continues to serve as the primary source of asphalt.

Figure 2-1 *The familiar asphalt parking lot. No other paving material approaches the total area of asphalt installed in the built environment.*

It is commonplace to hear asphalt criticized for its admittedly banal visual qualities and its impact on stormwater drainage and runoff. The familiar musical lament, *"They paved paradise and put up a parking lot,"* was directed squarely at asphalt and served as an indictment of the vast acreage of paving that accompanied an increasingly mobile population throughout the twentieth century. However, the widespread use of asphalt, particularly for roadway and parking-lot pavements, must be viewed as an utterly predictable response to the proliferation of the automobile and driver demand for safer, more convenient, and better engineered travel. We drive our cars on asphalt and we park them on asphalt when we're finished. Without the automobile, only a small fraction of the paved area that is currently covered by asphalt would exist. The economy, functionality, and maintainability of asphalt have jointly secured its place among exterior paving options, and organizations such as the Asphalt Institute are actively engaged in research directed toward enhancing its visual qualities and environmental performance.

CHARACTERISTICS OF ASPHALT

Asphalt is similar to concrete in many ways. Both are essentially conglomerates of aggregate materials (sand, stone, gravel) cemented into a hardened mass. Both are installed in a flexible, noncured state that strengthens over time. Concrete relies on water-activated cement for strength, whereas asphalt employs sticky petroleum-based binders known as *bitumens*; hence the name bituminous concrete. Bitumens offer a distinct advantage over water-activated cements in that they retain a degree of structural flexibility that is absent in the more brittle, fully cured concrete. This inherent flexibility eliminates the need for expansion and control joints, saving time and money during installation.

New asphalt pavement is laid in a heated mixture known as *hot-mix asphalt (HMA)*. The temperature of the binders in hot-mix asphalt exceeds 300°F and the mix must be placed and compacted before it cools to 185°F. Layers of hot-mix asphalt are laid down (spread) in horizontal *courses* which are in turn compacted by rolling to enhance the density and smoothness of the surface. As the installed mixture cools, it sets into a durable, homogenous paving mass.

Bitumens—the thick, black-to-brown viscous binders in asphalt pavements—are derived from petroleum. As petroleum is a limited natural resource, this fact carries with it a wide range of economic and political issues that accompany oil and petroleum acquisition, both domestically and globally. A more practical concern over bitumens is the potential for surface degradation due to vehicles leaking or spilling their own petroleum-based pollutants onto a bituminous surface, where they act as solvents on the asphalt mix. Concrete is typically introduced as a paving material in the immediate area of gasoline pumps, truck docks, or other areas that are prone to petroleum spills and drips.

As with concrete, the placement and curing of asphalt requires a specific temperature range. In general, it is best to place asphalt in ambient air temperatures above 40°F. Thinner courses that are less than 1½ inches thick may require even warmer ambient temperatures.

STANDARDS

Asphalt pavements that support vehicular traffic require the placement of multiple courses (layers) of asphalt, each with its own "recipe." When each of these courses includes asphalt binders, the resulting pavement is known as *full-depth asphalt*, a configuration preferred by the Asphalt Institute. Each course differs in its proportion of binder to aggregate, as well as the size of aggregate specified.

Vehicular asphalt pavements that carry medium to heavy traffic loads call for full-depth HMA design and require three courses above a compacted earth subgrade. The bottommost course is called the *base course*. The base course is placed directly on compacted earth. It features the highest ratio of aggregate to binder—up to 90 to 96 percent aggregate—and calls for the largest aggregate size range. This course is the thickest in section, typically about 25 mm or 10 inches. The *intermediate course* is also called the *binder course*, and the visible top course is known as the *surface course* or *wearing course*. The thickness of the intermediate course will be about 19 mm or 7½ inches. The mixture of the thin (9.5-mm or 3¾-inch) surface course calls for the highest proportion of binder and uses a finer aggregate to create a smooth driving surface.

Driveways and small parking lots carry lighter traffic loads at lower speeds than roadways. They require only a base course of 6 to 8 inches of aggregate, such as crushed stone, topped by a 2-inch (after compaction) surface course. A 2-inch hot-mix asphalt base course can be substituted for the aggregate base course. Individual courses of paving asphalt for light traffic areas are typically specified as about 1½ inches in thickness after compaction.

Individual state departments of transportation develop and maintain approved specifications for vehicular paving and any associated aggregate courses. Many designers simplify the design process by relying on the relevant state standard(s) to guide the configuration and components of their paving details.

DECORATIVE ASPHALT

The term *decorative* describes a variety of treatments that address asphalt's primary design drawback: its general lack of visual interest or richness. Colors, textures, and patterns not typically associated with hot-mix asphalt are available to designers. These treatments entail additional labor and materials, so they do not come without a cost. However, decorative asphalt still falls below the installed cost of true masonry unit pavers, giving designers a cost-effective alternative.

For *aggregate bonding*, the surface course of hot-mix asphalt is impregnated with an aggregate selected by the designer. The bonding of the aggregate to the asphalt can be achieved in a variety of ways. The aggregate can simply be applied and then rolled into the warm surface course. A more durable finish results from the use of epoxy binders, which create a strong bond between the aggregate and the asphalt. Aggregate impregnating creates a homogenous, uniform surface that takes on the color and texture of the aggregate. Because the colors are derived from aggregates rather than dyes, they tend to be organic and naturalistic.

With *imprinted asphalt*, a jointing pattern is pressed (imprinted) into the surface of still-hot or reheated hot-mix asphalt. Available patterns mimic

Figure 2-2 *Asphalt is not limited to use in parking lots. Uniquely colored aggregate was specified to give this walkway a more appealing appearance.*

Figure 2-3 *This stamped asphalt pattern simulates the look of cut stone pavers at a fraction of the installed cost.*

a wide range of masonry patterns. The resulting pavement combines the visual interest of unit pavers with the even surface and low maintenance of asphalt. Patterns can also be imprinted on newly applied surface courses laid over existing pavements, giving designers the option of reusing in situ stable pavements as base courses.

Thermal fusing systems employ a durable thermoplastic that is fused into the surface of hot-mix asphalt to create patterns and shapes. A recess is first formed in the surface of the asphalt, much like imprinting. This recess is then filled with thermoplastic that fuses to the surrounding asphalt. The resulting surface is flush and relatively easy to maintain. Thermal fusing is recommended for high-traffic pavements.

In *color coating*, color is applied as a component in a durable, wear-resistant coating applied over the surface of the asphalt. The colors available vary by manufacturer, but range from naturalistic simulations of brick and stone to more vivid primaries and pastels. Colors are available with solar reflectance indexes (SRIs) that help to minimize the localized "heat island" effect of urban areas.

"GREEN" ASPHALT

As discussed earlier, asphalt materials are not typically associated with sustainable site planning. Indeed, asphalt is often viewed as the very antithesis of ecologically friendly development. Responsible designers need sound strategies to exploit the proven benefits of asphalt while mitigating its more negative

environmental characteristics. Landscape designers can employ a number of effective measures to minimize the environmental impacts associated with asphalt paving:

- Porous asphalt offers significant environmental benefits over traditional asphalt pavement. As its name suggests, porous asphalt allows water to drain through voids in its mass and to percolate into the subgrade, rather than flowing quickly over its surface into overtaxed stormwater collection systems. At least three measurable environmental benefits accrue from the use of porous asphalt: the *rate* at which stormwater enters the drainage system is slowed; the *volume* of water classified as runoff, versus that which percolates into the soil, is reduced; and the *quality* of the water is enhanced through the partial removal of suspended solids, metals, oil, and grease inherent in parking lot and roadway runoff.
- To the eye, porous asphalt appears similar to standard asphalt, but with a slightly coarser texture. This is a result of the voids present in its composition, which permit rapid percolation.

The visible surface course of a porous asphalt installation is classified as "open-graded." Despite appearances, the surface course is smooth enough to satisfy the requirements of the Americans with Disabilities Act (ADA).

- The heart of a porous asphalt pavement is its stone recharge bed, a course of large, well-graded crushed stone whose mass is approximately 40 percent void. The uniform size of the aggregate in this course is critical. Poorly graded or "dense-graded" mixes include a wide variety of aggregate sizes all the way down to fines. Such a mix tends to fill the voids between the larger stones, tremendously slowing water infiltration. The maintenance of voids over the life cycle of a porous pavement is the key to its performance. It is important that the earth subgrade supporting the porous asphalt retain a good rate of percolation by omitting the traditional compaction undertaken during installation. The stability typically afforded by the compaction of the subgrade is compensated for by increasing the overall thickness of the stone recharge bed.
- Porous pavements have been in use only since the mid-1970s, so widespread measures of long-term

Figure 2-4 Porous asphalt paving is an effective option for managing stormwater runoff and water quality issues associated with impervious pavements.

performance and durability are lacking. Though small, the sampling of early installations indicates few cracking or pothole problems and the continuation of effective rates of infiltration.

- "Warm-mix" asphalt represents an attempt to reduce the relatively high temperatures associated with the production and placement of hot-mix asphalt. Warm-mix asphalt requires temperatures that are between 30° and 100°F lower than traditional hot mix asphalt. The benefits of warm-mix asphalt include reduced energy consumption, lower emissions of greenhouse gases, and reduction of the all-too-familiar fumes and offensive odors that accompany hot-mix installations.

- The technology of warm-mix asphalt is relatively new, spurred by international agreements to reduce greenhouse gases. The primary challenge facing the development of warm-mix asphalt is to achieve qualities of strength and durability that equal or surpass those inherent in hot-mix asphalt, while significantly enhancing environmental performance.

- Designers can call for light-colored asphalt to help mitigate the "urban heat island" (UHI) effect. Dark pavements and roofs store daytime heat and release it at night. Air pollutants are inevitably present within the trapped heat island domes that encase urban areas, significantly reducing air quality.

The concentration of stored heat along with diminished air quality in urban areas predictably results in increased reliance on energy-consuming air conditioning. Lighter-toned surfaces do a better job of reflecting solar radiation while dispersing heat and airborne pollutants.

- Light-toned, heat-reflecting surfaces are also one of several key components in achieving LEED certification for a project's site work. Leadership in Energy and Environmental Design awards points, under its Sustainable Sites credit area, for improving a site's solar reflectance index (SRI). SRI is a measure of the ability of a surface to reflect rather than store solar radiation.

- Virtually 100 percent of demolished asphalt can be recycled into new asphalt. Designers can do their part by insisting that project specifications require recycled content to be used in all proposed asphalt paving installations.

- Perhaps the biggest impact designers can have lies in physical site configuration, particularly in the layout of roads, parking, or any other impervious site paving. Well-planned and efficient circulation systems not only improve environmental performance, but also reduce site development costs in the process. Most zoning ordinances permit a percentage of "small-car spaces," which require less surface area than traditional spaces. The advantageous location of small-car spaces can motivate users and employees to drive smaller, more fuel-efficient vehicles. A project's parking program should establish a realistic, workable number of off-street parking spaces while satisfying zoning codes. Where applicable, designers should consider parking configurations that take advantage of opportunities for shared parking. As an example, movie theaters are busiest in the evenings and on weekends, whereas the need for parking to service professional offices peaks during the day, from Monday through Friday. If these two uses are strategically sited within a mixed-use development, a significant percentage of their respective parking spaces could be shared, reducing the total area of paved surface needed. Progressive zoning ordinances acknowledge these use-specific patterns and permit reduced parking requirements where the potential for shared parking exists.

ASPHALT BLOCK UNIT PAVERS

Much like precast concrete unit pavers, asphalt block unit pavers are produced under controlled factory conditions. This offers many distinct advantages over hot-mix asphalt. The units are visually and characteristically consistent, as they are not subject to variations in climate, weather, and jobsite conditions. Colors and finishes are available that are not possible with hot-mix asphalt. Color, size, shape, and unit scale yield opportunities for greater visual interest, expanded design options, and a more human-scaled feel than large areas of homogenous, undifferentiated HMA. Walkways composed of hexagonal asphalt block pavers are familiar to users of New York City's Central Park, where years of traffic and wear have resulted in a slight "turtle-back" profile, much like granite cobblestones. Some manufacturers' asphalt block pavers contain a percentage of postindustrial recycled content, enhancing their green credentials without detracting from performance.

Asphalt block unit pavers are available in a variety of shapes and attractive organic colors, depending on the manufacturer. Grades and thickness range

Figure 2-5 *Compared to other masonry unit pavers, asphalt unit pavers offer a durable and cost-effective paving option.*

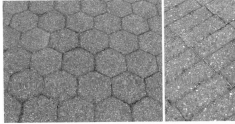

Figure 2-6 *Asphalt unit pavers are available in a variety of shapes and sizes. The familiar hexagonal paver remains a popular choice.*

from residential to commercial to industrial. Their petroleum-derived base component resists becoming brittle at low temperatures, minimizing the potential for cracking. It also yields excellent water resistance and low absorption. The finish of asphalt blocks can be left smooth, which highlights the darker color of the binder, or ground to reveal the colors of the component aggregates and give the pavers more surface texture. As with precast concrete pavers, manufacturers continue to explore new finishes and textures.

The installation of asphalt block pavers does not require mortar or any other form of joint sealant. Pavers are laid "hand-tight" over either flexible (aggregate or sand), semirigid (hot-mix asphalt), or rigid (concrete) bases, typically employing an asphalt setting bed.

Figure 2-7 The hexagonal asphalt unit pavers in this installation nicely complement the more costly granite and brick pavements.

The design advantages of asphalt block pavers do not come without cost. Their installed cost per square foot easily exceeds the economies yielded by hot-mix asphalt, being more comparable to a flexible brick or a precast concrete pavement.

DRAWING STANDARDS

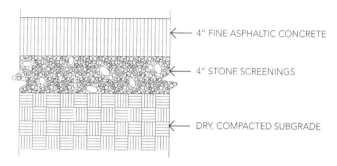

← 4" FINE ASPHALTIC CONCRETE

← 4" STONE SCREENINGS

← DRY, COMPACTED SUBGRADE

Figure 2-8 Light-duty asphalt is best used for low-intensity applications such as walks, trails and residential driveways.

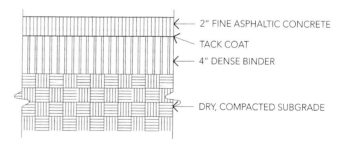

← 2" FINE ASPHALTIC CONCRETE

← TACK COAT

← 4" DENSE BINDER

← DRY, COMPACTED SUBGRADE

Figure 2-9 Heavy-duty asphalt is needed to support higher traffic volume and heavier vehicles.

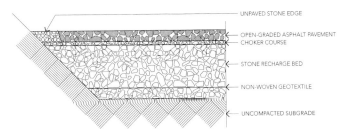

UNPAVED STONE EDGE
OPEN-GRADED ASPHALT PAVEMENT
CHOKER COURSE
STONE RECHARGE BED
NON-WOVEN GEOTEXTILE
UNCOMPACTED SUBGRADE

Figure 2-10 Porous Asphalt Detail.

LEARNING ACTIVITIES

1. Locate the Website for the National Asphalt
   Pavement Association.
   a. Locate, read, and summarize a technical report
      dealing with environmental asphalt performance
      for materials such as porous asphalt or cooler
      asphalt mixes (warm-mix asphalt).

2. Locate the Website for a manufacturer of asphalt
   block unit pavers.
   a. Summarize the shapes, dimensions, and
      finishes available from that manufacturer.
   b. Identify the compressive strength in pounds
      per square inch of the pavers.

GENERAL

Brick is a tried-and-true staple of the human-made landscape. A member of the masonry family, it is strong, durable, and attractive. Its small unit size gives landscape designers tremendous flexibility in creating pattern, form, texture, shadow, detail, and visual interest. Its color is derived naturally based on the precise composition of the parent clay, which yields rich, organic tones.

Even though brick is not quarried like stone, its raw materials (primarily clays and sometimes pulverized shales) are excavated from deposits in the earth. Thus, brick can provide a poignant expression of *genius loci* (sense of place). Brick has never fallen out of style. It has survived ever-shifting stylistic preferences, and consistently been a material of choice for designers.

Figure 3-1 This brick wall achieves depth, shadow, and visual interest by using a sawtooth arrangement in which each brick is set at 45 degrees.

Building Brick versus Paving Brick

Brick is ideal for both horizontal landscape applications, such as pavements, ramps, and steps; and horizontal uses, such as walls, columns, pillars, and bollards. It is important, though, for designers and material specifiers to understand the significant differences between paving brick and building brick. Vertical brick structures are exposed to water and the elements only during storms and the period of drainage that immediately follows a storm. Horizontal brick installations are far more exposed to the effects of standing water, snow and ice, freezing and thawing cycles, chemicals used for de-icing, chemicals that drip from vehicles, and the constant stresses of traffic loads.

To survive in such a challenging environment, a brick paver must be stronger, denser, and more water resistant than a building brick. It would be a costly mistake to use building bricks for a paving installation. An all-too-frequent client request is that salvaged historical building bricks be reused for a patio, driveway, walkway, or terrace. No building brick should be used for paving; older building bricks are even weaker than those manufactured today, and thus deteriorate that much faster.

CHARACTERISTICS OF BRICK

Like most masonry materials, brick is strong in compression and relatively weak in tension (i.e., it is *brittle*). Given the proper support, though, brick pavements can support the heaviest of loads. It is very difficult to squash a brick, but when brick is placed in a spanning condition with no support beneath, it is very likely to snap or crack. This structural trait is frequently exploited by martial arts experts seeking a dramatic demonstration of their skills (although they are unlikely to use *paving* bricks for their demonstration!).

The compressive strength of even light traffic paving bricks is between 7,000 and 8,000 pounds per square inch (psi) of surface area. This compares to a typical range of 3,000 to 4,000 psi for typical exterior concrete pavements. When properly detailed and installed, a brick pavement is a viable alternative for almost any landscape situation, regardless of the anticipated load.

Both mortared (rigid) and hand-tight (flexible) pavements expand and contract with temperature changes. Rigid pavements contract and expand as a single, integral mass; in contrast, the numerous joints within a flexible pavement accommodate horizontal and vertical displacement. All brick pavements, but especially rigid systems, must provide for expansion, or the weakest material constituting the system will likely fail. The failure may occur in the mortar joints, any surrounding rigid containment, or within the brick itself.

STANDARDS

ASTM

The standard ASTM specification for building brick is designated as C 62. Finished facing brick is covered under designation C 216. Most landscape paving brick is governed by ASTM Designation C 902, *Standard Specification for Pedestrian and Light Traffic Paving Brick.*

Brick pavers are sometimes shunned in favor of concrete or asphalt because their actual dimensions may vary from brick to brick after firing. It is argued that this slight dimensional variation complicates snow removal and other maintenance operations. The acceptable variation of individual brick units is governed by ASTM. The field supervisor must be aware of the acceptable range in unit size and has the authority (assuming that the project has a properly worded set of written specifications) to reject any brick units that fall outside of the ASTM specified range. Designers and specifiers will find this information in tabular form under *Tolerance on Dimensions, Maximum Permissible Variation from Specified Dimension, plus or minus.*

Other key brick characteristics addressed by ASTM specifications include maximum permissible chippage, maximum allowable cold-water absorption, abrasion requirements, and acceptable warpage of individual units.

Standard Nomenclature

The term *brick* is often applied to any building material that is bricklike in shape, size, and proportion. For the purposes of this text, a *brick* is defined as a building or paving unit composed primarily of fired clay or pulverized shale. The process of firing brick in a kiln at extremely high temperatures is a key step differentiating brick from sun-dried clay units such as adobe. During firing, brick undergoes a molecular transformation known as *vitrification,* a process also important in the manufacture of ceramics. In contrast, adobe is simply dried and hardened clay. Vitrification imparts strength and water resistance to brick that significantly surpasses sun-drying. (Unit pavers and wall units resembling brick but composed of precast concrete are discussed in chapter 5). If it is the process of firing that differentiates brick from adobe, and the parent material that distinguishes brick from precast concrete units, it is *function* and *clay content* that differentiate brick from terra cotta. *Terra cotta* literally translates as "fired earth." Its composition is similar to that of brick in many ways, but terra cotta contains a higher percentage of pure clay and is typically used for more ornamental or decorative molded shapes.

Brick has a long and rich tradition that can be traced back thousands of years. Although standardized sizing for brick units arrived only recently, there exists a long-established nomenclature describing the various qualities and techniques of working with brick.

As with most masonry building materials, a horizontal layer of brick is called a *course.* Vertical brick elements are laid in *courses.* Most permanent vertical brick construction involves *mortar,* the cementitious material that bonds the bricks while providing structural support. The interface between brick and mortar is called a *joint.* Joints in vertical brickwork account for approximately 17 percent of the exposed surface area, making them important visual components in the overall design of a brick wall or pavement. Mortar is an optional and sometimes undesirable element in brick pavements. The intense stresses placed on horizontal pavers are also at work on horizontal mortar joints. The breach of a mortar joint can seriously compromise the integrity of a paving system by allowing water to penetrate into base courses.

A *wythe* is an Old-World term still in common use. It is defined as a single *width* (see following discussion on dimensioning) of brick in the context of a vertical brick wall. Exterior landscape walls are often composed of two wythes, with header bricks (bricks that span across the wythes) bonding the wythes together at specified increments. Today, the most common wythe dimension is nominally 4 inches.

Size and Dimensions

The dimensions of bricks are noted in a consistent sequence: width, height, and length (also denoted

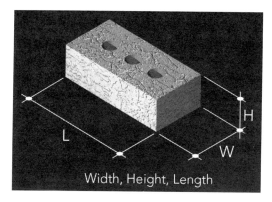

Width, Height, Length

Figure 3-2 The standard designation of a brick's nominal or specified dimensions is given in width, height, and length.

WHL). Brick sizing can be confusing. Bricks have three distinct sets of measurements: actual size, specified size, and nominal size. Designers need only be concerned with nominal size. Specified or targeted size and actual size after firing are the concerns of brick manufacturers and brick masons.

The Brick Industry Association (BIA) has established a widely adapted set of standard sizes for both building and paving brick. The standardization of brick unit sizes occurred only within the twentieth century and has tremendously facilitated the accurate translation of designers' working drawings in the field.

Wall Positions

A brick has six faces, and thus six possible orientations within a brick wall. Designers can incorporate these positions in combinations to create visual interest and to create structural bonding of vertical wythes. Varying arrangements of stretchers and headers have given rise to the various traditional bond patterns, such as English bond, Dutch bond, and Flemish bond.

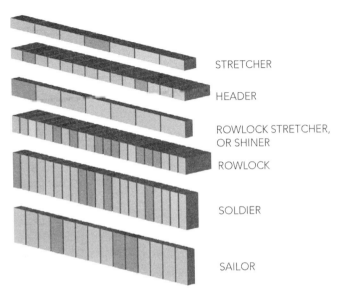

STRETCHER

HEADER

ROWLOCK STRETCHER,
OR SHINER

ROWLOCK

SOLDIER

SAILOR

Figure 3-3 The six possible orientations (positions) of brick within a wall.

Cored Bricks and Solid Bricks

When designing vertical brick landscape elements, designers will most likely be using cored building or facing brick. Core holes allow more even firing, as the heat from the kiln can penetrate into the core of

Figure 3-4 Exposed core holes detract from an otherwise well-crafted serpentine wall.

the brick. They also serve as "keys," creating better mortar bonds between adjacent bricks. Core holes reduce the overall raw material needed to manufacture the brick and reduce its shipping and handling weight. They do not diminish the structural capacity of a brick in any measurable way, but they can be unsightly when exposed in a finished surface.

Bricks may be designated as "solid" and yet have core holes. This invariably leads to a certain amount of confusion when a designer specifies *solid* bricks with the actual intent of specifying *noncored* bricks. A brick may be designated as a solid unit provided the surface area of the core holes does not exceed 25 percent of the load-bearing surface area of the brick itself. Designers should take care to specify the necessary quantity of noncored bricks for use on wall ends and caps, or in any situation where the core holes would otherwise be exposed. Cored bricks are not appropriate for use as pavers.

Classification of Brick

Exterior brickwork is constantly exposed to the unrelenting forces of nature. The ASTM has established

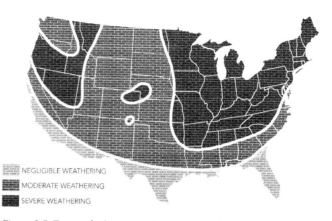

NEGLIGIBLE WEATHERING
MODERATE WEATHERING
SEVERE WEATHERING

Figure 3-5 *Zones of relative weather severity in the United States.*

three weathering zones for the United States based on the degree to which localized weather events work to degrade brick. The zones range from Negligible Weathering (NW), to Moderate Weathering (MW), to the most severe zone, Severe Weathering (SW). These designations apply to building brick whether it is used in a building or a more exposed landscape situation. NW brick should not be considered for a landscape application. Many landscape designers will specify only

SW brick for their projects, particularly in the northern two-thirds of the United States.

Paving brick features its own system of classification. The degree of exposure replaces the degree of weathering, and is based on anticipated continued exposure to the elements. SX refers to brickwork placed in a location where severe exposure is likely, as defined by the probability of freezing while saturated with water. Class MX (moderate exposure) may be used in southern climates where freezing is not expected, and Class NX brick (negligible exposure) should be used only for interior installations.

The Modularity of Brick

It has been noted earlier that the actual size of bricks will vary after firing, as a result of the varying degrees of moisture present in the parent material that is burned off during firing at extremely high heat. Designers need not concern themselves with the actual size of bricks unless the bricks fall outside of the ASTM's permissible variation range. Rather, designers should prepare working drawings showing only the *center*

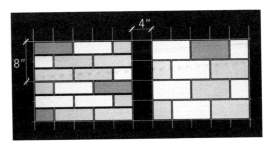

Figure 3-6 Modularity in brick detailing is based on a 4-inch grid for both vertical and horizontal (paving) installations.

lines of the desired joints. Thanks to the modularity of brick and the national standardization of sizes, there exists an implicit understanding between designers and installers. Properly trained bricklayers will accommodate any (acceptable) variations in brick dimensions simply by making slight adjustments in the size of the mortar joints. A useful aspect of the currently accepted standardized sizes is that they are modular based on a unit of 4 inches or multiples of 4 inches. Vertically, the joint center line above and below three courses of standard brick stretchers will measure exactly 8 inches, even if the individual bricks vary slightly. The

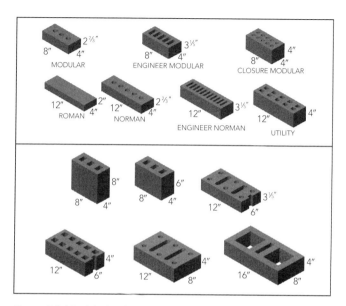

Figure 3-7 Modular brick sizes with nominal dimensions.

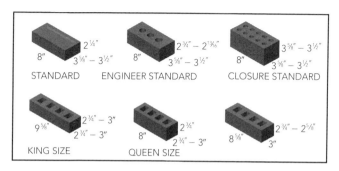

Figure 3-8 Nonmodular brick sizes with their specified dimensions.

horizontal mortar joints of stretcher bricks will also occur at precisely 8-inch increments (for standard brick), and 4 inch increments for header bricks.

The modularity of brick sizing expedites the production of working drawings, but it has another distinct advantage as well. Brick cavity walls often utilize concrete masonry units (CMUs) for interior support. CMUs are less costly than brick and can perform the same structural role. The center lines of the vertical joints of CMUs conveniently occur at 8-inch increments, and the horizontal joints occur every 16 inches. Both are multiples of four, ensuring that the joints of every third course of brick will align precisely with one course of concrete masonry units, facilitating the installation of the necessary mechanical ties linking the brick to the supporting block.

Thanks to the modularity of brick, the designer can work within a planning grid of 4 inches to accurately and quickly detail the desired configuration of a brick wall or pavement. Working drawings that feature the outlines of each individual brick waste both time and money without achieving any greater clarity or accuracy.

BRICK CONFIGURATIONS

Despite the unlimited freedom and creativity that designers enjoy when configuring brick, several tried-and-true arrangements for brick pavements and walls have evolved. These patterns have stood the test of time and continue to enjoy widespread use. Some designers simply replicate these layouts; others use them as starting points for more original expressions.

Brick Pavements

There are four types of brick pavements. Their designation depends on two factors: the presence or absence of mortar in the joints, and the type of base course used for support. Brick pavements with mortared joints are designated *rigid* paving systems. All rigid paving systems must be configured using rigid base courses of concrete. Nonmortared pavements are also called *flexible* paving systems. In these applications, the bricks are laid hand-tight and water is permitted to move through the system. Flexible paving systems can be placed on a variety of bases depending on the need for durability, stability, and strength. For heavy-traffic commercial installations, a flexible system placed on a rigid base (concrete) is recommended. For residential pedestrian brick pavements, a flexible base configured of aggregates and sand may suffice. An intermediate level can be achieved using a semirigid base course (asphalt). All four systems call for a setting or leveling bed between the brick course and the base course. Rigid paving systems should not be installed above flexible or semirigid base courses.

Rigid paving systems function on the premise that they create an impervious membrane to water. All drainage flows across the surface, to be collected by either mechanical drains or topographical drainage features such as swales or basins. Rigid systems work well until the integrity of the mortar joints is breached.

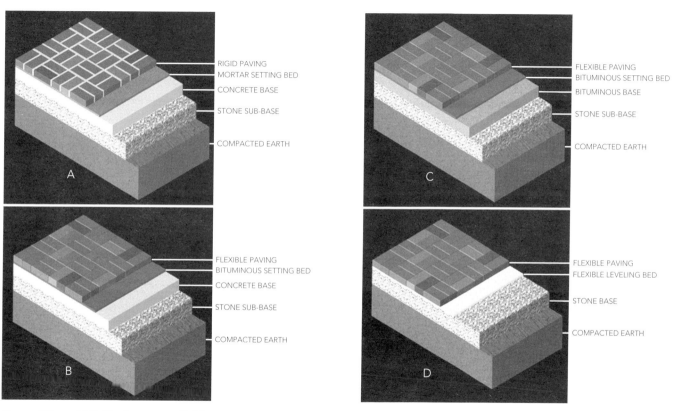

Figures 3-9a and 3-9b The four types of brick pavements.

A

RIGID PAVING
MORTAR SETTING BED
CONCRETE BASE
STONE SUB-BASE
COMPACTED EARTH

B

FLEXIBLE PAVING
BITUMINOUS SETTING BED
CONCRETE BASE
STONE SUB-BASE
COMPACTED EARTH

C

FLEXIBLE PAVING
BITUMINOUS SETTING BED
BITUMINOUS BASE
STONE SUB-BASE
COMPACTED EARTH

D

FLEXIBLE PAVING
FLEXIBLE LEVELING BED
STONE BASE
COMPACTED EARTH

Water that penetrates the surface and is allowed to settle and to freeze and thaw can have a devastating impact on the integrity of the pavement. Rigid pavements that are improperly graded and permit standing water have an equal likelihood of failure. Rigid pavements expand and contract as a single entity. Great care must be taken to calculate and provide adequate expansion capability within the system itself and wherever the rigid pavement meets another rigid element, such as a building, wall, or curb.

Flexible pavements have no mortar or any form of bonding between the individual units. The pavers move independently rather than as a single unit. If rigid pavements are analogous to peanut brittle, flexible pavements are like a handful of peanuts. It is anticipated that water will penetrate the surface of a flexible pavement and that drainage will be provided for. For flexible pavements supported by impervious base courses, drainage must be provided both at the surface level and at the level of the impervious base course, to minimize water retention. Flexible pavements atop flexible base courses have the advantage of facilitating drainage directly through the entire system into the subgrade.

Paving Patterns

Designers and their clients often select a particular brick paving pattern based on visual preference alone. Although visual interest is an important benefit of brick, aesthetics should not overshadow its more subtle structural characteristics. Flexible brick pavements under vehicular traffic loads are susceptible to slippage, especially along long, uninterrupted linear joints. This is particularly true of joints that run parallel to the direction of traffic. Designers should scrutinize paving patterns to identify the longest linear joints. In the common running bond, all the joints in one axis run the entire length of the pavement, whereas the joints in the other axis are never longer than the width of the brick itself (typically 4 inches). This pattern has a much greater tendency to slip along the long, uninterrupted joints than along the shorter, staggered ones. Thus, designers should orient the longest joints *perpendicular* to the direction of traffic.

While evaluating the patterns in Figure 3-11 for their longest linear joints, note that the herringbone pattern has no linear joints longer than one length plus one width of a paving brick. Individual bricks in this pattern have a high degree of *interlocking*. The stacked bond is the least stable or interlocked, with long joints running in both axes. And the popular basket weave pattern is in reality just a variation of the stacked bond pattern.

Any of the patterns shown in Figure 3-11 can be installed with the joints rotated 45 degrees to the perimeter. This measure can add visual interest and will orient the joints somewhat away from the direction of traffic, but it also will add to the labor cost and the material waste resulting from cutting the numerous perimeter bricks.

Joint orientation is not a significant factor when designing pedestrian-only pavements such as patios or garden walks. The stresses of foot traffic alone are not substantial enough to cause significant slippage. In these situations, the decision as to pattern and configuration can be based largely on visual characteristics and preferences.

Brick Walls

Three basic types of brick wall are used in landscape applications. The most traditional is the solid

Figure 3-10 *Brick paving remains more stable in vehicular traffic when the longest joints are oriented perpendicular to the direction of traffic.*

masonry wall. As the name suggests, these walls are composed entirely of brick. There are no cavities internal to the wall, nor is there a secondary material (such as concrete) behind the brick surface. The most common configuration of solid masonry brick walls is a double-wythe wall with the necessary bonding headers.

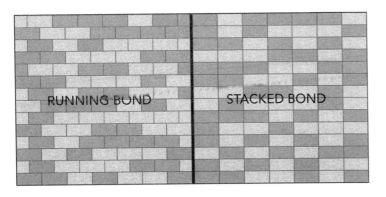

RUNNING BOND   STACKED BOND

HERRINGBONE   BASKET WEAVE

Figure 3-11a

Modified basket weave patterns

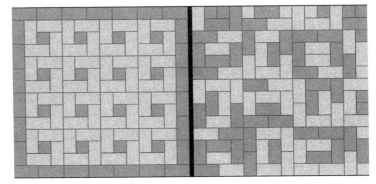

Figure 3-11b

Custom patterns

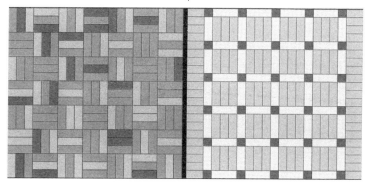

Figure 3-11c

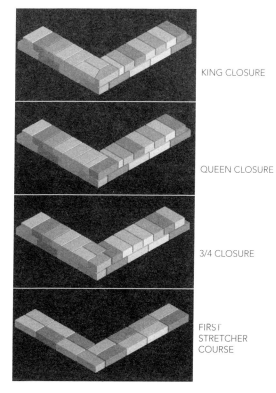

KING CLOSURE

QUEEN CLOSURE

3/4 CLOSURE

FIRST
STRETCHER
COURSE

Figure 3-12 Three alternatives for turning a 90-degree corner in solid brick wall construction.

A double-wythe wall will result in a wall thickness of approximately 8 inches. Often designers desire a wall of greater thickness, for use as a seat wall or simply for visual reasons. Simply adding more wythes (and additional bricks) may be an inefficient means of achieving the targeted dimension. The internal, unseen component of such a wall is better achieved using concrete masonry units or cast-in-place concrete. The concrete is encased in brick, with the brick face mechanically tied to the backup material. To facilitate installation and drainage, a minimum of 2 inches is called for between the brick and the concrete, giving rise to the designation of these walls as *cavity walls*. Cavity walls must deal with the inevitable fact that water will penetrate into the cavity; hence, a means of drainage must be provided. Drainage can be facilitated by using mechanical vents, by installing rope wicks, or simply by having nonmortared head joints at regular intervals in the lowest brick course.

Wall Bonds

As discussed earlier, a double-wythe wall requires header bricks placed at regular intervals to structurally

Figure 3-13 *Typical construction of a brick cavity wall with a concrete masonry unit backup.*

bond the two wythes together into a single unit. Thus, the visible face of the wall is some configuration of stretchers and headers. A number of traditional bond patterns have evolved over time, each tracing its heredity back to its own geographical origins. Terms like English bond, Dutch bond, and Flemish bond refer to the preferred arrangement of stretchers and headers among masons in each region. The advent of steel frame construction in the building industry relegated exterior brick walls to a veneer role instead of a structural one. As a result, header bricks became obsolete. The traditional bond patterns disappeared from the designer's palette and were nearly lost to antiquity. As postmodern designers rediscover the various bond patterns, there is a risk that the patterns will be evaluated purely on visual terms. Bond patterns can indeed impart significant visual interest, but their primary role has always been to provide structural stability. Although it is unlikely that we will see the return of structural, load-bearing brick walls in architectural applications, traditional bonded brick walls continue to have a place in the designed landscape.

A third type of landscape wall is the *perforated wall*. Perforated walls may also be called *pierced*

Figure 3-14 *A mechanical vent allows moisture to escape from the interior of the wall.*

walls or *brick screen walls*. Perforated walls give the designer the benefits of the beauty and stability of brick while permitting light and air into an exterior space. A perforated brick wall is, in effect, functioning as a fence in the landscape. These walls are best used when absolute privacy is not a requirement, although

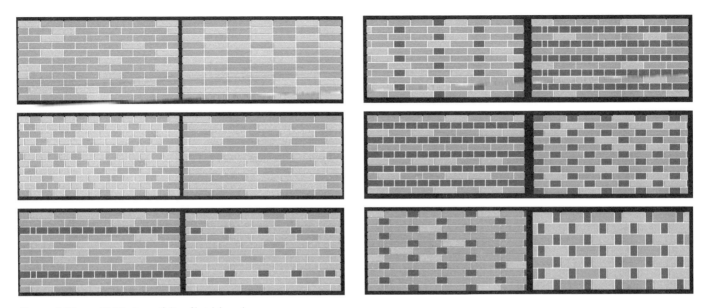

Figures 3-15a and 3-15b A portfolio of brick bonds.

the thickness of a double-wythe brick wall makes visual access surprisingly difficult.

As with paving patterns and wall bonds, there are a number of traditional perforated wall configurations and there is the opportunity for wholly original arrangements. Many of the traditional perforated patterns are achieved simply by removing some or all of the header bricks from a bond pattern. The voids

Figure 3-16 Perforated brick walls provide privacy and security while permitting light and air into an outdoor space.

Figure 3-17 The voids in this perforated brick complement the architecture in the background.

resulting from the removed headers create a pattern with significantly more contrast than a bond pattern. The depth and shadow inherent in a perforated wall make a strong visual statement. However, because the absent headers served an important bonding function, the designer must provide some other means of tying the wythes together, such as mechanical ties.

Standard Finishes

The majority of brick manufacturing today uses the stiff-mud process, in which brick is shaped by extruding unfired clay through a die. To achieve slip resistance and for visual purposes, manufacturers may apply a finish to one or more faces of the brick. Traction is particularly critical for paving brick.

After brick is extruded through the die, it must be cut into individual units prior to firing. This is achieved through the use of cutting wires set at the mouth of the die. The cutting process provides an opportunity to impart a texture to the brick. Manufactures have evolved a range of terms to describe the finish of their bricks. Designers will encounter terms such as *velour, scratch, rug, bark, rockface, sandface, stippled, striated, molded, matte,* and *smooth.* Each finish has its own unique visual characteristics. Manufacturers sometimes describe their brick finishes creatively, using nonstandard nomenclature. Designers should never specify a brick finish or color without first examining a comprehensive range of samples.

Drawing Standards

When detailing brick for construction documentation, the universal graphic method is to infill the brick with a diagonal hatch pattern, as shown in Figure 3-18.

When preparing plan views or wall elevations, indicate only the center lines of the joints.

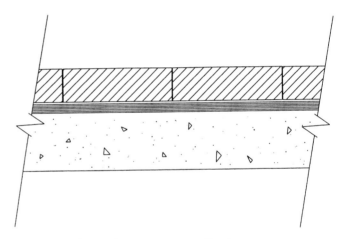

Figure 3-18 *The graphic representation of brick in construction documents.*

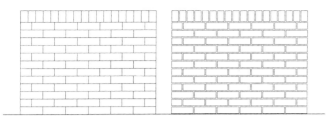

Figure 3-19 *Correct detailing of brick walls portrays the center lines of the joints, not the individual bricks.*

Do not spend needless time or energy drawing the outlines of the individual bricks. Masons installing brickwork use a *story pole* in the field, which is marked with the modular locations of these same joint center lines.

Mortar Joints

The total area of mortared joints in a typical brick wall comprises approximately 17 percent of the surface of the wall. Simply put, the role of mortared joints is to bind the individual brick units into a structurally sound unit. From a designer's perspective, however, the joints also serve other functions beyond mere adhesion. In both vertical and horizontal applications, brick joints serve at least two other primary purposes. Studies reveal that the overwhelming majority of masonry failure occurs at the joints. The mortar joints in a brick installation must provide effective protection from the forces of the weather, especially water resistance, as standing water is particularly detrimental to brick construction. Additionally, the depth and profile of mortar joints serve an important design role in the overall visual appearance of a wall. The joint design in a skillfully crafted masonry installation represents a balancing act of form and function that must accomplish both of these ends equally well.

To achieve resistance to weather, a well-tooled joint must prevent water from remaining in the joint. Given adequate time, water can work its way into a joint and ultimately degrade the bond between the mortar and the masonry unit. Once this bond is defeated, a cycle of failure ensues. In cold climates, freezing action on any standing moisture hastens the failure of the joint.

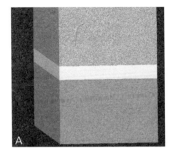

Figure 3-20a Flush.

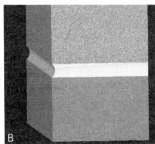

Figure 3-20b Concave.

Figure 3-20e Grapevine.

Figure 3-20f Raked.

Figure 3-20 Typical mortar joints.

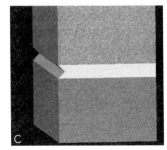

Figure 3-20c V-shaped.

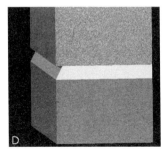

Figure 3-20d Weathered.

COMMON PROBLEMS AND MITIGATION MEASURES

As with most landscape materials, problems with brick can arise from three sources: faulty manufacturing, inadequate installation, or improper detailing. Only the latter is within the control of the designer. At the risk of oversimplification, the designer should first and foremost address issues related to drainage. Expediting proper and rapid drainage from brickwork will prevent the majority of typical failures associated with this material.

Efflorescence

One of the most frequently heard complaints related to finished brickwork is efflorescence. *Efflorescence* is a whitish residue deposited on the surface of finished masonry. It is caused by water interacting with soluble salts commonly present in the parent clay. The problem does not lie with the salt content of the clay, but in the prolonged contact of water with the brick that causes the salts to leach to the surface. Efflorescence should be viewed as a symptom more than a problem. It is an indicator that water is present internal to the brickwork and is not draining adequately. Although efflorescent deposits can be removed, they are likely to reappear if the underlying source of the water is not eliminated. Vertical brick walls with caps or copings that drain poorly invite water into the brickwork and can lead to efflorescent deposits.

Spalling and Cracking

Spalling is the flaking away, or *exfoliating*, of the outer surface or crust of a brick. Spalling and cracking are signs of undue stress on finished brickwork.

Figure 3-21 *Good materials can fail when poorly detailed or installed. The lack of expansion joints either caused or contributed to the failure of this brick paving.*

Spalling is indicative of internal stresses, such as the freezing and thawing of water or the expansion of soluble salts. It is likely to occur when building bricks are used as pavers, or when paving brick does not meet ASTM standards for strength and water absorption.

Poor drainage is not the cause of spalling brickwork, but it is certainly a catalyst for spalling. Cracking suggests that brick has been placed under tensile stresses. Culprits may include a failed or insufficient base course or inadequately designed expansion joints. A distinct advantage of flexible brick paving systems is the relatively easy replacement of cracked or spalled bricks. Nevertheless, replacement is no more than a stop-gap solution until the source of the failure is resolved.

ADVANCED BRICKWORK

In the hands of skilled designers and craftworkers, brickwork can be elevated to rich, artistic expression. Over the lengthy history of brick in the built environment, a number of techniques have evolved to enhance the beauty and visual interest of brick. Designers can employ these techniques while remaining safely within the structural limitations of brick by understanding and using some simple formulas.

Corbeling

In architecture, a *corbel* is simply a decorative bracket that projects from the face of a wall. It is achieved with brick using a reverse stair-stepping effect. Each course

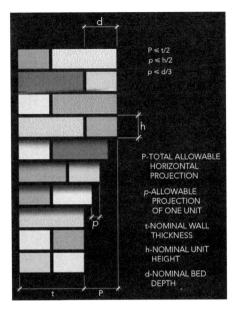

Figure 3-22 Corbels can create depth and shadow. Their stability results from a few simple structural guidelines.

of brick within a corbel is cantilevered out from the course below. By adhering to the guidelines shown in Figure 3-22, designers can ensure that the bricks are not placed under excessive tensile stresses.

Diapering

Diapering is an Old-World term indicating diagonal patterns in brick created by using headers, contrasting brick colors, or both. Diapering patterns can be subtle or bold, depending on the degree of contrast. Although the labor needed on the part of the mason to install a diaper is increased, the visual effect can be dramatic. Simple diapering patterns can be achieved by using contrasting brick in standard bond patterns such as Flemish or Dutch bonds.

Serpentine Walls

Serpentine walls exploit the flexibility of brick's small unit size, combining gracefully meandering curvilinear forms with the strength and durability of brick. Their pattern of reversing curves provides stability by utilizing the principle of corrugation. For minor serpentine landscape walls (walls 4 feet or less in height), the mathematics of corrugation are simple. As curves become shallower and radii become larger, the wall approaches a straight line and thus begins to lose the structural benefits of corrugation. These guidelines serve to ensure adequately deep curves and sufficiently

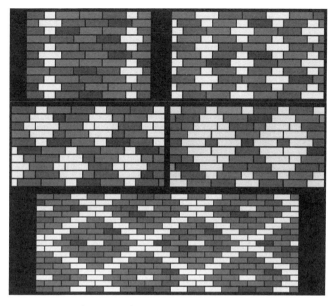

Figure 3-23 *Bricks creatively arranged in patterns with contrasting colors can yield an unlimited range of diapering patterns.*

tight radii. The radii should not exceed twice the height of the wall and the depth of curvature should be no less than one-half that same height measurement. There should be no section of tangent wall between

Figure 3-24 Serpentine brick walls gain structural stability through use of the principle of corrugation.

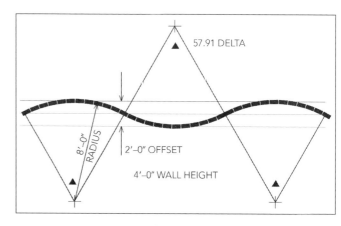

Figure 3-25 Layout geometry for serpentine walls.

the reversing curves. So, for a wall with a height of 4 feet, the radius should not exceed 8 feet and the depth of curvature should be at least 2 feet.

Quoins

Quoins are an ancient method of visually strengthening the corners or turns within a wall. Historically, quoins

were stone units, but brick can be effectively used to create quoins, as shown in Figure 3-26. Greater emphasis can be placed on the quoins by using a contrasting brick color.

Saw Tooth

Saw tooth, also known as *dog's tooth*, is a simple way to add dramatic visual interest to brickwork. It is surprisingly

Figure 3-26 Corner quoins composed of contrasting bricks are an economical way to create visual interest.

simple to achieve and adds relatively little to the cost of a brick wall. The bricks in a sawtooth course are simply rotated 45 degrees to the face of the wall. Each successive course is staggered and oriented perpendicular to the

Figure 3-27 Bricks are simply rotated 45 degrees to achieve the sawtooth courses in this otherwise featureless wall.

preceding course. The resulting pattern adds depth and shadow to an otherwise flat wall surface.

Sculpted Brick

Sculpted, or carved, brickwork is an artistic yet labor-intensive process of shaping individual bricks before firing. It is somewhat misleading to simply categorize sculpted brick as costly masonry. From a design perspective, sculpted brick represents an economical means of producing hand-made sculpture when compared to hand-sculpted stone.

The most common method of producing sculpted brickwork is called *intaglio*, a process in which the design is incised into the face of unfired, noncored standard brick. The unfired brick is temporarily assembled into a panel and sculpted while still green. The sculpting of unfired brick requires considerably less effort than the carving or chiseling of stone. Once the sculpting process is complete, the individual bricks are coded according to their row and course to facilitate reconstruction. After the panel is disassembled, the bricks are kiln-fired and permanently reassembled on site. Another method of creating

Figure 3-28 *Sculpting brick while still green adds enormous potential to its use as a decorative element.*

sculpted brickwork entails chiseling the brick after it is fired, usually on site, then assembling it into the final sculpture.

Craftsmanship in Brick

Brick masons associated with the order of Teutonic Knights raised brick construction to an exceptionally high level during the medieval period. These masons apparently acknowledged no bounds as they pushed brick to the most expressive level imaginable. Examples of their craftsmanship survive to the present, serving as testament to the utility, durability, and visual beauty of this material.

Figure 3-29 Brick has a deep history of craftsmanship in the built landscape.

SUPPORTING ORGANIZATIONS AND RESOURCES

Detailing and installing brick correctly is far more economical than doing repairs or replacement after the fact. A number of organizations exist to assist designers in developing sound details for brickwork. One such organization is the International Masonry Institute.

To quote their promotional material, "IMI offers design and technical assistance and will help you find skilled craftworkers in all of the trowel trades. IMI is a labor/management cooperative of the International Union of Bricklayers and Allied Craftworkers and the Contractors who employ its members." The International Masonry Institute sponsors an impressive number of educational programs, targeted to craftworkers, engineers, and designers. The International Masonry Institute will discuss technical questions over the telephone, or via its Internet site.

The International Masonry Institute
Internet address: http://www.imiweb.org/

The International Masonry Institute also maintains regional and area offices across the country; each of these offices can provide assistance with design and engineering questions.

Another important organization is the Brick Industry Association (formerly Brick Institute of America). In a document entitled, INTRODUCTION to the BRICK INDUSTRY ASSOCIATION, the role of the BIA is neatly defined: "BIA is the national trade association representing distributors and manufacturers of clay brick and suppliers of related products and services. The Association is involved in a broad range of technical, research, marketing, government relations and communications activities. It is the recognized national authority on brick construction."

"The mission of the Brick Industry Association is to serve the united interests of the brick manufacturing industry, primarily: to render technical assistance to designers and others; to provide marketing assistance to the industry; to monitor and positively influence governmental actions; to assure the long-term availability of bricklayers; and to provide other member services, as appropriate. BIA's programs are designed to accomplish objectives which either cannot be achieved by the members themselves, or are more efficiently carried out collectively."

It is difficult to imagine a masonry-related article, book, or publication that does not cite BIA's Technical Notes as a primary source of information. The BIA's continuing efforts to disseminate reliable technical information on masonry design have led to the development of a CD-ROM based version of Technical Notes, and, more recently, a user-friendly Website containing useful technical design data and links. The Brick Industry Association also publishes the color periodical, Brick in Architecture, which occasionally features site-related installations. The significant contributions made by the BIA have earned it the unofficial title of "the national authority on brick construction."

Brick Industry Association
Internet address: http://www.bia.org/

LEARNING ACTIVITIES

1. Research and select one of the standard brick bond patterns.
   a. Using a scale of 1 inch = 1 foot-0 inches, prepare an elevation of a double-wythe brick wall that is 8 feet long and 4 feet high.
   b. Using the same scale, prepare a section through your wall which cuts through the headers.

2. Select a brick paving pattern such as basket weave or herringbone. (Students may alternatively choose to configure a unique pattern of their own design.)
   a. Using a scale of 1 inch = 1 foot-0 inches, prepare a plan detail of your walkway.
   b. Using the same scale, prepare a detail section through your walkway. Select a system using a rigid, semirigid, or a flexible base.

CHAPTER **4** **CAST-IN-PLACE CONCRETE**

GENERAL

Concrete enjoys a well-deserved reputation as a strong, durable, and affordable material. Unlike its aggregate-based cousin, asphalt, concrete is not limited to horizontal or paving applications, and thus is employed in a far greater variety of applications in the built landscape. Concrete is the human-made material that comes the closest to achieving the strength of natural stone, so it is not surprising that it is used for many of the same landscape applications. Cast-in-place concrete is delivered to a jobsite in a liquefied form, often called "ready-mix concrete," and is poured into formwork, taking its shape in the process. This gives concrete a distinct design advantage over unit masonry, in that it can take on virtually any shape or configuration that can be created with forms without the costly and time-consuming cutting otherwise needed with rigid unit masonry.

Figure 4-1 Cast-in-place concrete arrives at the site mixed and ready to pour into formwork.

Concrete is frequently misidentified by novices as *cement*. Concrete and cement are not synonymous. Cement is an ingredient in concrete. One dictionary defines *concrete* as "joined in or constituting a mass."*

Cement is one of the components joined into that mass. The other ingredients in a basic concrete mix include sand, stone aggregate, and water. When the cement is activated (crystallized) by water, it bonds, or "cements" the ingredients into a homogenous, coalesced mass.

The use of concrete does not date as far back as brick or stone, but predates asphalt by a wide margin. The Romans' use of concrete is well documented. Egyptians and Greeks also used concrete-like mixes. Early concrete recipes used cements derived from naturally occurring ingredients such as clay, lime, and gypsum. The story of modern concrete dates to 1824, when an English inventor and brick mason, Joseph Aspdin, was granted a patent for his invention of Portland cement. Modern concrete mixes still employ his cement, which is created by burning a combination of calcium, silicon, aluminum, and iron; the process yields a fine powder that is activated by water. It is perhaps ironic that concrete made from Portland cement is considered "hydraulic" (i.e., activated by water), yet when it is fully cured the resulting concrete is highly resistant to water.

In addition to water, Portland cement, sand, and aggregate, another element is commonly incorporated into concrete: steel reinforcing. Although concrete is extremely strong, cured cast-in-place concrete is also quite brittle. Steel, ranging in size from flexible no. 10 welded-wire mesh to large-diameter reinforcing bars (rebar), provides additional strength and resiliency.

CHARACTERISTICS OF CAST-IN-PLACE CONCRETE

Cast-in-place (CIP) concrete is employed in pavements, walls, steps, and a wide range of site furnishings where strength, durability, and economy are factors. It is used both as a finish material and in a less visible backup role, providing structural support for other veneer or finish materials. Once cured, it is highly water-resistant,

*Funk & Wagnalls Standard Dictionary of the English Language, 1958 by Funk & Wagnalls Company, combined with Britannica World Language Dictionary, 1959 by Robert C. Preble.

making CIP concrete an ideal choice for footings and foundations, where it is typically accompanied by structural steel.

CIP concrete pavement is a familiar element in the human-made landscape. Both strong and affordable, poured concrete is an excellent choice for large paved areas where the budget precludes the use of costlier unit pavers. The cured strength of a CIP pavement is typically between 3,000 and 4,000 pounds per square inch (psi).

As with asphalt, the placement of CIP concrete is temperature sensitive. Admixtures can adjust the curing time of the mix and permit the pouring of concrete within a wider temperature range. In addition to temperature, CIP concrete is vulnerable to all the variables associated with an exterior construction site, including precipitation, workmanship, and batch consistency. An all-too-common complaint by designers concerns a section of sidewalk poured at the end of one work day that fails to match the adjacent section poured the next work day. Even though these two pours may meet the same technical specifications, they may have been mixed in separate batches, have been delivered in different vehicles, and have been

Figure 4-2 Pedestrian safety is a critical requirement in the design of landscape steps. Concrete steps with concrete footings are both safe and stable.

installed by different crews. Even the weather can vary from one day to the next, subtly altering the look of the cured concrete. It should come as no surprise that it is often difficult to match adjoining pavements poured on different days.

Cast-in-place concrete requires physical containment, called *forms*, to maintain its shape until it is cured. The installation of forms can represent a significant component of the labor-related cost, especially if the desired shape is complex. Concrete formwork has evolved to facilitate installation, helping to minimize labor, and can be reused for many cycles. Some forms can even impart a textured or patterned finish to the surface of the concrete.

AMERICAN SOCIETY FOR TESTING AND MATERIALS

The American Society for Testing and Materials (ASTM) promulgates several standards dealing with cast-in-place concrete and many of its components mentioned in this chapter:

ASTM C94—Specification for Ready-Mix Concrete
ASTM C979—Pigments for Integrally Colored Concrete
ASTM C150—Portland Cement

ASTM C33—Concrete Aggregates
ASTM A185—Welded Wire Fabric Reinforcing
ASTM C143—Slump Testing for Cast-in-Place Concrete

In addition to the ASTM standards, specifications for cast-in-place concrete often refer to standards established by the American Concrete Institute (ACI), found under ACI301, *Specifications for Concrete.*

STANDARDS

For cast-in-place concrete pavements, it is the responsibility of the designer to specify the thickness of the slab, along with the materials to be used, the compaction of the base, the subbase, the concrete finish, and any form of reinforcing to be incorporated into the slab. It also typically falls to the designer, via the technical specifications, to specify the materials to be used in the formwork and the method of installing the formwork, both of which can dramatically affect the final appearance of a concrete installation. Concrete pavements typically range from 5 to 8 inches in thickness, depending on the anticipated traffic load. A commonly used section for a pedestrian walkway would be 5 inches of concrete, with a grid of no. 10 welded-wire mesh that has a mesh spacing of 6 inches in both directions. On a construction detail, this reinforcing would be noted as "6 x 6 No. 10 WWM." To minimize movement resulting from frost heave and soil moisture, concrete should be placed over 6 inches of compacted and leveled aggregate, such as crusher-run stone or road-base aggregate. To further enhance overall stability and to minimize the potential for subsequent settling, the earth subbase must also be leveled and compacted. Most professional design offices maintain digital libraries of details that they have found to be successful in their region.

Where vehicular traffic is anticipated, the thickness of the CIP concrete section should be increased to 6 inches for driveways and residential garage floors, or 8 inches for roads, parking lots, or truck docks. Concrete is like most masonry materials in that it is strong in compression and relatively weak in tension. It is the role of the aggregate base and the compacted subbase to ensure that the concrete slab remains in a compressive condition. Settling or erosion of

Figure 4-3 *The contrasting color of this concrete identifies it as a bicycle lane.*

the subgrade can place a rigid slab of concrete in a spanning, or tensile mode, where it is only a matter of time until a significant surface load cracks the brittle material. Provided the base and subbase are properly compacted and remain intact, the concrete installation can successfully support extremely heavy loads.

Jointing Cast-in-Place Concrete

One of the most significant differences between cast-in-place concrete pavements and asphalt pavements is the need for jointing. Because of its bituminous base, asphaltic cement maintains a higher degree of flexibility than concrete. The cement in concrete is activated by water. When fully cured, only a negligible amount of water remains in the concrete, resulting in a loss of flexibility. Thus, when thoroughly cured, concrete is extremely rigid and brittle. Given the normal temperature variations that accompany seasonal changes, as well as daily solar cycles, a slab of concrete pavement will measurably expand and contract as a whole unit along its entire mass. This movement can wreak havoc on adjacent construction materials and within the structure of the slab itself. Hence, this movement must be accommodated using a system of internal joints. There are two types of joints with which designers are primarily concerned: control joints and expansion joints.

Control Joints

Concrete is prone to cracking. During curing, as it dries and hardens, concrete can shrink about 1/16 inch

Figure 4-4 Control joints are technical necessities, but represent opportunities for creative expression.

for every 10 feet of length. This shrinkage results in tension within the curing concrete that makes cracking a strong likelihood. Large, wide cracks can be hazardous and allow water into the structure of the pavement, resulting in an accelerated cycle of failure. Even fine cracking is unsightly. Control joints are the designer's tool for controlling where internal cracking will occur. Control joints, sometimes referred to as *contraction* joints, are intentionally weak locations within a concrete slab. When appropriately placed, they will not prevent the concrete from cracking, but will successfully dictate where that cracking occurs. An effective control joint must create a line in the concrete that is sufficiently weaker than the surrounding concrete so as to give the crack few choices. To accomplish this, the depth of a control joint should be no less than one fourth the depth of the slab. A control joint that is too shallow will give a developing crack too great an opportunity to migrate out of the joint and determine its own path.

A second key consideration in the design of control joints is their spacing, or *frequency*. If the spacing is too great (if they are too far apart), they may indeed invite and host cracking as intended, but additional

Figure 4-5 *Good jointing design does not prevent concrete from cracking. Rather, it works to control where the cracking will occur. This crack in a pedestrian sidewalk was caused by an unanticipated and extreme vehicular load.*

cracks are likely appear elsewhere in the slab. For linear walks, 8 feet is typically the recommended maximum spacing between control joints. Many designers use more stringent spacing, such as 5 to 6 feet for greater

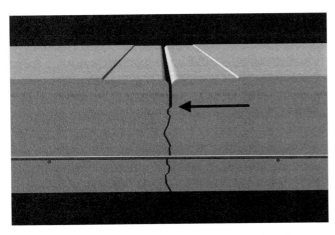

Figure 4-6 *The depth of an effective control joint must be at least one-fourth of the total concrete thickness.*

Hand-tooling with a grooving or jointing tool is the most common method of creating control joints in concrete slabs. Maintaining a precise arrangement of straight, parallel, and perpendicular joints calls for a degree of skill on the part of the installer. Even the most experienced worker should employ a system of straightedges to guide the joints. A second method of installing control joints involves cutting the cured concrete with a power saw fitted with an abrasive or diamond-embedded blade. "Saw-cut" joints are crisper and more precise than hand-tooled joints, but the nature of the bulky power tool (particularly its circular blade) makes it difficult to employ where the pavement meets vertical elements such as walls or curbs. In these circumstances, it is impossible to complete the joint to the edge of the pavement.

Expansion Joints

Expansion joints are highly flexible and resilient materials placed between any two nonflexible (rigid) materials, including cast-in-place concrete. An expansion joint is needed in a concrete pavement wherever the pavement abuts another rigid material, such as a building

assurance; however, it must be kept in mind that the installation of more closely spaced joints requires additional labor, which translates into some additional cost to the project. For broad, nonlinear concrete pavement areas where the pavement width exceeds 20 feet, the width of pavement contained within control joints should not exceed 20 feet.

foundation or slab, wall, curb, or simply more concrete slab. Imagine a site where a concrete pavement abuts a rigid building floor slab. On a warm day, both pavements will expand in dimension. Without an expansion joint, the two slabs will exert tremendous pressure on each other, until one or both fail, resulting in cracking or fracturing. The role of an expansion joint is to absorb those dimensional changes, creating a zone into which each slab can expand without encountering the other.

If this were the only function required of an expansion joint, the joint could simply be configured as a void between two rigid elements. An effective expansion joint must also remain debris-free and watertight. It must remain pliable and intact through multiple freeze thaw cycles and seasons. A number of materials are used as expansion joints. Historically, asphalt-impregnated fiber or felt was used; this material is still available and effective. More recently, premolded, elastic, resilient materials have been developed that are resistant to water and have longer functional life spans than organic materials. To prevent water infiltration into the slab, the joint should be sealed with flexible caulking formulated specifically for exterior concrete applications. A well-designed

Figure 4-7 *Thoughtful layout and configuration of control joints adds interest and meaning to concrete paving. Here, the linear patterns play a significant supporting role in an overall design concept.*

expansion joint should also include a foam backer rod situated between the joint material and the sealant. Unlike control joints, which run partially through the slab, expansion joints must run the full width of the concrete to perform adequately.

The thickness of an exterior expansion joint is typically between ¼ inch and ⅝ inch. No exterior expansion joint should be narrower than ¼ inch. To accurately estimate the amount of expansion (in inches) that will occur in an exterior concrete slab, multiply the slab length in inches by the number of degrees (Fahrenheit) of anticipated temperature variation by a factor (called the *coefficient of expansion*) of 0.0000055. As an example, a 50-foot (600-inch) slab, in a region where the temperature is expected to vary from –10 degrees in the winter to +90 degrees in the summer (a range of 100°F), yields an anticipated expansion of 0.33 inches (600 x 100 x 0.0000055). Knowing the anticipated dimension of expansion enables designers to specify for the appropriate joint thickness and spacing. In general, thinner joints spaced at more frequent intervals offer better control than thicker expansion joints spaced at longer intervals.

Dowel-and-Sleeve Joints

A dowel-and-sleeve joint is used in concrete slabs where it is necessary to maintain a level surface between adjacent concrete elements. This joint does not necessarily prevent vertical displacement, but rather works to prevent *differential* vertical displacement. Examples are where a walkway meets the top or bottom of a set of cast-in-place concrete steps, a ramp, or where an exterior paving slab meets a building slab or foundation. In this joint, a series of evenly spaced rigid steel dowels spans between the two rigid elements. Any vertical movement that does occur can only occur in both elements simultaneously, preventing a trip edge from emerging. These locations are nearly always locations where expansion joints are also needed, so it is critical that the dowel-and-sleeve joint do its job without obstructing any necessary horizontal movement. To do this, the rod must be allowed to move independent of the concrete on at least one side of the joint. This is accomplished either by lubricating the surface of one end of the rod or by wrapping it in a material that can serve as a bond breaker between the steel rod and the concrete.

Design Implications of Control Joints

Incising a pattern of linear joints into a concrete slab carries obvious design implications, beyond the more technical role of controlling cracking. The configuration of control joints should be a carefully conceived part of the overall design. The thoughtful placement of control joints can result in rhythms and a sense of visual movement. Jointing patterns are an effective means of breaking down the scale of large paved areas. Designers must consider the overall form, scale, and geometry of the concrete slab along with the geometry of surrounding contextual elements. It is best to resolve control joints as close as possible perpendicular to the edge of the concrete slab. Placing acute angles in a concrete pavement, especially near its perimeter, yields thin wedges of brittle material that will tempt unwanted cracks.

FINISHING CAST-IN-PLACE CONCRETE

This section addresses horizontal installations such as pavements, ramps, and step treads, as well as vertical installations such as walls and columns. Providing an attractive and sound finish is an essential step in both types of concrete installations, but they entail different approaches. Although both types of cast-in-place concrete installations require formwork, only horizontal applications permit complete access to the primary, visible surface while it is still wet and as it cures. The forms used in vertical applications prevent access to the primary surface until the concrete is cured and the forms are removed.

Horizontal (Flatwork) Finishes

As with all exterior pavements, safety is a primary factor in selection of a surface finish. Concrete can be floated and trowelled to yield an impressively smooth finish. This may be appropriate for the floor of your garage or basement, but it can be quite slippery in outdoor applications, especially when wet. It is almost always preferable to finish the surface with a texture that will provide traction and slip resistance. No two pedestrians are equally able-bodied. Those with physical limitations, the elderly, toddlers, expectant mothers, or simply individuals wearing stylish but unstable footwear need all the traction a pavement can offer. It is advisable to err on the side of safety when selecting the surface finish for any pavement.

Figure 4-8 The broom finish of this concrete walk adds texture and safety to the walking surface. The alternating direction of the striations must be specified by the designer.

Float and Trowel Finishes

Hand-floated and trowelled finishes are created as the cast-in-place concrete pavement is curing. Craft workers can employ a variety of trowels, depending on the pattern and texture desired. Metal trowels

composed of steel or aluminum generally impart a smoother surface, whereas wooden trowels create more texture. Experienced finishers can create distinctive patterns of arcs or swirls in a surface, or can achieve smoothly floated, featureless surfaces.

Broom Finish

The most common finish for exterior cast-in-place concrete is called a *broom finish*. Its name derives from the use of a wide broom to *consistently* impart fine linear striations into the surface of the concrete. These striations in turn create a slip-resistant texture. It is not sufficient for designers to simply label a cast-in-place detail section with the flag "Broom Finish." Because a broom finish is also a significant visual design element of the pavement, it falls to the designer to provide as much information as is necessary regarding the direction and orientation of the pattern of striations. It is typical to orient the striations perpendicular to the direction of traffic flow. This makes any waves or irregularities in the striation pattern less apparent to the eye. Another common approach is to alternate the direction of the broom finish between perpendicular and parallel, changing direction at the pavement control joints. In broader paved areas, this 90-degree alternation imparts a checkerboard effect.

Exposed Aggregate Finish

An attractive finish available for cast-in-place concrete pavements involves exposing some portion of the aggregate used in the concrete mix. Aptly named *exposed aggregate*, this finish elevates the aggregate to a lead role in the pavement design. There are two basic methods for exposing stone aggregates in a cast-in-place installation. In the first, most common method, aggregate is exposed at a critical moment during the curing process, by removing some depth of the surface of the concrete. Alternately, the desired aggregate may be broadcast over and rolled into the surface, so that it becomes embedded in the curing concrete. In both methods, skill and timing are key factors in the success of the final appearance. Regardless of method used, an exposed aggregate finish represents an extra measure of labor and thus increases the cost of the pavement.

Figure 4-9 Exposed aggregate concrete paving provides an opportunity to enhance the color and texture of cast-in-place concrete.

As with a broom finish, designers should not leave the final appearance to chance. With the constituent aggregate playing such a critical role in the overall appearance of a pavement, it is incumbent upon the designer to carefully select and specify the aggregate

Figure 4-10 Stamped concrete, combined with surface coloration, can yield attractive and rich concrete paving.

for its color, texture, consistency, and scale. At its best, an exposed aggregate finish combines the warmth, richness, and visual interest of stone aggregates with the strength and durability of concrete.

Stamped Concrete

Although it has been available for decades, stamped concrete is gaining considerable favor among designers. Once considered "artificial appearing," methods have evolved for achieving increasingly realistic colors, textures, and patterns in stamped concrete, giving designers and their clients cause to reconsider its merits. Virtually any pattern that can be achieved using traditional masonry pavements, from herringbone brick to random flagstones, can be convincingly achieved with stamped concrete.

Stamped concrete is a finish that is applied while the concrete is still wet. The concrete slab is poured into forms and leveled as any other cast-in-place concrete slab would be. Then, while the concrete is still plastic, the specified pattern is stamped into its surface. Advances in patterning have allowed for a greater degree of randomness in "stone" patterns. Whereas no two stones are identical in true stone pavements, early stamping patterns were analogous to wallpaper patterns, in that there was a predictable and fairly noticeable repeat of pattern elements. The development of keyed patterns allows greater choice among any two adjacent stamps. As long as the "keys" at the edge of any two stamps fit together, the stamps may be paired and will yield a continuous, unbroken pattern. This allows for a degree of randomness by eliminating some of the predictability of the pattern.

Despite much refinement and enhancement in the process and appearance, stamped concrete is essentially one material aspiring to imitate something else. This invariably raises concerns among designers who disdain even a hint of artifice in their projects. In the end, it falls to individual designers to determine the appropriateness of stamped concrete within the parameters of a particular project, given the client, the budget, and the physical and historical contexts.

Rock-Salt Finish

For a rock-salt finish, salt crystals $\frac{1}{8}$ inch to $\frac{3}{8}$ inch in diameter are broadcast onto newly poured concrete. The salt crystals are pressed into the

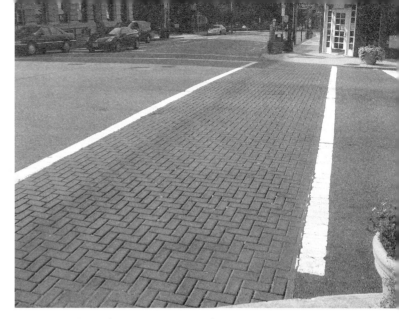

Figure 4-11 *This pedestrian crosswalk is defined by a distinctive stamped concrete brick herringbone pattern. The change in color, pattern, and texture communicates both the pedestrian and vehicular zones.*

concrete using a roller. After the concrete is cured, the surface is washed; this process dissolves the salt and leaves a texture of small pits and holes in the surface.

Figure 4-12 Broom-finished concrete combined with stamped concrete simulating masonry unit pavers.

Figure 4-13 A distinctive pattern in cast-in-place concrete achieved through the use of contrasting admixtures.

Coloration

Coloration of concrete is an effective way to elevate a somewhat mundane and ubiquitous landscape element into something with much more visual interest and richness. Frank Lloyd Wright employed dyed concrete almost exclusively as the flooring material in his Usonian homes. Colors in concrete can be achieved with a number of methods, or by combining two or more methods. For consistency and uniformity of color, a dye can be mixed into the concrete mix itself. A distinct advantage of integral color is that it cannot wear away under weather and traffic like a surface applied dye, since the coloration exists evenly throughout the mix. However, this also means that a significant percentage of the dye is buried deep in the slab where it will never be seen.

Few materials produced by nature display even and consistent coloration throughout. A more variegated color effect in concrete can be achieved by applying colorant to a slab surface using broadcast dyes or acid washing. By carefully varying the intensity of the broadcast colorant, interesting mottled and organic appearing tones can be achieved. Even more effective color treatments of cast-in-place concrete result by combining admixtures with surface treatments. The more translucent and variegated surface applications complement the solid-color admixtures to create depth and realism.

Sealing Concrete

As with most hardscape paving materials, sealing the surface of concrete is an added option available to designers. Sealing provides protection against water and the elements, as well as resistance to staining.

Sealed concrete appears rich and lustrous, almost wet, much like the result when a coat of glossy varnish or polyurethane is applied to wood. The seal can be either clear or color-tinted to enhance standard ready-mix concrete or to complement colored concrete. Slip resistance can also be added to the sealant to improve overall safety.

The sealing of concrete represents an additional step, so it is an additional installation cost to the client. The surface coat of sealant will have to be replaced or redone periodically, perhaps every 3 to 5 years, so clients need to be made aware of ongoing maintenance requirements.

Vertical Finishes

Even though the concrete mixes may be quite similar, the approach to vertical cast-in-place applications is fundamentally different from approaches to horizontal ones. Formwork for pavements rarely retains the visible, exposed surfaces of a slab. The horizontal (formed) sides of paving slab are nearly always buried beneath finished grade, while the exposed surface is finished using one or more of the methods described earlier in this chapter. The formed surfaces of a wall, in contrast, are highly visible after the formwork is removed. Thus, the formwork itself plays a much more integral role in the finishing of the wall or vertical application. Also, because the formwork cannot be removed until the concrete is fully cured, none of the finishing options available for wet or partially cured concrete pavements can be used on walls.

Form Finish

The term *form finish* applies to the exposed finish of a wall created by the forms themselves. This is easily the least costly and simplest method of finishing a vertical concrete pour, but it is the most difficult for the designer to control and to achieve predictable or desirable quality. Unless the designer has called for specific forms that create a desired texture or pattern, the final finish is subject to the variables and characteristics of whatever the contractor used to form the concrete. Wet concrete flows into any and all surface voids. Low-grade plywood forms will imprint a negative of their surface texture and irregularities directly into the wall. This may be acceptable for industrial applications or areas like truck docks or service bays, but may be too crude for more public landscapes. Despite the contractor's best attempts to fully fill the forms, unwanted air pockets and voids can occur even when the mix has been thoroughly vibrated. These voids do not become evident until the wall has cured and the forms are removed. Unsightly patching, which rarely matches the surrounding wall, is often the only way to fill these voids. Walls poured on different work days or poured using different batches may also fail to match. Seams are another potential source of inconsistency in form finished walls. When not properly sealed, seams may dry and cure faster than the rest of the wall, leaving a noticeable difference in color, or they may ooze wet concrete, resulting in raised fins or ridges of concrete.

Given the myriad of visual inconsistencies that can arise with cast-in-place concrete walls and their formwork, a variety of methods have evolved to hide, mitigate, or eliminate surface problems.

Sandblasting

Sandblasting, as the name suggests, is a finish treatment in which grit is sprayed onto a wall under high pressure and at high velocity, removing a *specified* amount of the wall's external surface. In the process, sandblasting imparts a sandpaper-like texture to the wall, as it softens and mitigates any flaws in the wall. Designers can specify light, medium, or heavy sandblasted finishes. Each designation specifies, within a set range, the amount of surface material to be removed by the sandblasting process. Removal of the outer "crust" of concrete by sandblasting exposes some of the aggregate used in the mix. This adds interest and changes the overall hue of the finished face. It can also serve to mask some of the imperfections inherent in form-finished concrete walls.

Bush-Hammer Finish

A bush-hammer finish can be thought of as an extreme sandblast finish. Instead of blasting the wall with grit, bush-hammering utilizes a mechanical tool (hammer) that repeatedly impacts the surface of the concrete, creating a rough texture—significantly rougher than even a heavy sandblast finish. Bush-hammering is most frequently performed using a

pneumatic-powered tool, also known as an *air bush;* manual bush-hammers represent a less costly but more labor intensive alternative. The face of a bush hammer is dimpled which is key to achieving a random textured surface.

Bush-hammering will hide even the worst of forming flaws, but a bush-hammered surface is very rough and not particularly skin-friendly. As with the sandblast finish, the overall evenness and consistency of the surface depends largely on the skill and experience of the craft worker.

Form Liners

All of the finishing methods described in this section impart a finish to the concrete *after* it has cured significantly and the forms have been removed. Another approach is to line the formwork with reusable plastic or rubberized liners that have a specific pattern or texture on the inside surface. Wet concrete that is poured into the lined forms takes on that pattern or texture. The choices of pattern are limited only by commercial availability, and a vast array of patterns are available. Some seek to simulate other materials, such as brick or stone (cut or natural); others impart geometric, less representational patterns; and still other liners create nongeometric textures. Form liners are close cousins to stamped concrete pavement and carry many of the same benefits (economy, visual interest) and concerns (artifice, consistency). Much like stamped concrete, color and patina can be applied to wall surfaces, often using the same pigmented stains used for stamped concrete, to enhance realism and visual interest.

Form liners do not address the problem of air pockets or voids, and patching may be just as unsightly as on a form-finish wall. Nevertheless, form liners do represent an economical means of giving a cast-in-place concrete wall a custom appearance without using true masonry units such as stone or brick.

ENVIRONMENTAL CONSIDERATIONS OF CAST-IN-PLACE CONCRETE

One of the primary environmental concerns associated with traditional cast-in-place concrete is its lack of permeability and the resulting impacts on stormwater drainage and groundwater recharge. To address this concern, methods have been developed to permit water to drain or percolate freely through the concrete.

Pervious concrete pavement addresses the runoff issue by maintaining open voids that constitute between 15 percent and 25 percent of its volume. Stormwater drains vertically through the concrete pavement and percolates into the groundwater system rather than flowing across the pavement surface into a mechanical stormwater drainage system. The Environmental Protection Agency (EPA) recommends pervious cast-in-place concrete. Obvious benefits of pervious concrete include reduction of the volume and rate of stormwater runoff and enhancement of the water quality as it filters through the system. Another significant benefit of pervious concrete includes the reduction or elimination of project acreage that would otherwise be dedicated to retention ponds or drainage swales.

An environmental impact associated with concrete occurs long before the mix reaches the jobsite. One of the key ingredients in a concrete mix is powdered cement. Modern cements, including Portland cement, require extremely high heat—2,600°F to 3,000°F (1,430°C to 1,650°C)—to initiate the chemical reaction necessary to fuse the mix. These high temperatures require a tremendous consumption of energy, and the process thus represents a source of greenhouse gases. Although it may not be readily apparent as concrete is being poured into forms, the mix arrives with a significant amount of embedded energy.

To its credit, the aggregate materials employed in a concrete mix are not typically exotic but rather are locally available. Aggregate, sand, and water constitute much of the weight of a concrete mix. Much less energy is required to deliver to a jobsite a truckload of ready-mix concrete that originates from a local or regional source; this minimizes the energy consumption associated with long-distance transport.

Demolished concrete is suitable for recycling. It can be crushed and used as a road base or construction subbase aggregate mix. Portable, on-site crushers can further reduce the need to excavate and import aggregate material (natural resources) from quarries. The construction characteristics of recycled concrete compare favorably to those of crusher-run stone. Any rebar used in the demolished concrete is also a good candidate for recycling. American Concrete Institute (ACI) standard 555 deals explicitly with recycling concrete into usable aggregates.

LEARNING ACTIVITIES

1. Prepare a section through a cast-in-place concrete sidewalk; the section should be suitable for use as a construction document.
   a. Use a scale of 1 inch = 1 foot-0 inches.
   b. Use the following dimensions:
      - Concrete slab: 5 inches
      - Aggregate base: 6 inches
   c. Label all materials, including a compacted earth subbase.
   d. Indicate the desired surface finish of the concrete.
   e. Indicate and label 6 x 6 #10 welded-wire mesh.
   f. Include an appropriate title and reference symbol for your detail.

2. Develop a jointing plan for a cast-in-place concrete sidewalk. Keep in mind that technical solutions are also design opportunities.
3. Locate and photograph a problem or a failure in a CIP concrete pavement, such as cracking, settling, or poor finishing. Carefully examine the concrete and its surrounding context. Provide and defend your professional opinion regarding the specific cause(s) of the problem.

BOLLARDS

COLUMNS & PIERS

DRAINS & GRATES

FENCES & RAILS

PAVEMENTS, 1

PAVEMENTS, II

PAVEMENTS, III

SEATING, I

SEATING, II

SITE FURNISHINGS

STEPS, 1

STEPS, II

TREE GRATES

WALLS. I

WALLS, II

WATER

GENERAL

The recipe for precast concrete is very similar to that for cast-in-place concrete. Water is mixed with sand, aggregate, and cement, creating a fluid mixture that requires a mold or formwork to give the finished product its shape. That, however, is where the similarities between the two materials end. Precast concrete is manufactured under highly controlled conditions and is not susceptible to the unpredictable variations of the jobsite, the weather, and the workmanship. Its name derives from the fact that its preparation, or *casting*, occurs before (*pre*) it arrives at the jobsite. Precast concrete typically achieves levels of consistency, quality, strength, and finish that are difficult to approach with on-site cast-in-place concrete installations.

   Precast concrete is used in a wide range of applications in the landscape, but two areas of the market have seen notable growth in recent years: segmental retaining walls and unit pavers. The growing

Figure 5-1 Because of their strength, consistency, and relative economy, precast concrete pavers have enjoyed a tremendous growth in popularity.

popularity of precast concrete for these uses can be attributed to its significant cost savings over comparable options, along with its relative ease of installation.

Precast pavers are part of the larger family of *unit* (Individual) pavers. They are also referred to as *segmental* pavers. They are installed much like other unit pavers made from stone or brick. Precast pavers are considered economical within the spectrum of unit pavers, especially cut stone, but are generally more costly than hot-mix asphalt or cast-in-place concrete pavements.

Segmental precast paving systems date back to the late nineteenth century, when they were first employed in the Netherlands for roadway paving. The ability to mold precast pavers into a desired shape represents a distinct advantage over the relatively higher cost of cutting stone or brick pavers. This characteristic has been exploited to produce innovative shapes with interlocking faces that yield greater stability than straight-edged pavers and linear joints. Presorted kits of radial precast pavers have been developed, which allow designers to create circular paving patterns where the

use of stone or brick in the same configuration might be cost prohibitive.

CHARACTERISTICS OF PRECAST CONCRETE

Because of its durability, strength, and relative ease of forming, precast concrete is utilized in an enormous array of landscape applications. It may be the most widely adapted hardscape material currently available. The tremendous growth of use in retaining-wall construction reflects both economic and performance advantages. Its established niche as a paving material suggests a higher quality and greater visual interest than ordinary asphalt or cast-in-place concrete, but at an installed cost far less than brick or stone. Manufacturers of precast segmental pavers are quick to point out the high degree of consistency that can be achieved in their thickness, a trait that appeals especially to maintenance staff who are responsible for snow removal. Precast concrete pavers are also significantly stronger than cast-in-place concrete pavement. Whereas the latter typically achieves strengths of 3,000 to 4,000 psi, precast pavers can easily double that, while meeting or exceeding the absorption rate of paving brick.

High-quality precast concrete is a convincing substitute for limestone when used for copings, stair treads, or ornamental details. It is used extensively for pavements and walls, but it also excels in approximating the qualities of stone when used for planters, bollards, seating, and a wide array of other site furnishings. It is almost always more affordable than similar elements made from natural stone.

Segmental precast concrete systems that do not use mortar for adhesion of the units enjoy several advantages over their cast-in-place counterparts. Cracking is nearly nonexistent in segmental pavements or walls. Segmental precast retaining walls mitigate the destructive buildup of hydrostatic pressure by allowing groundwater to seep through their many flexible joints. However, segmental pavements do not necessarily eliminate the need for expansion joints. Figure 5-4 demonstrates the destructive force generated by a segmental precast pavement as it expanded against an

Figure 5-2 *12 × 12 precast pavers with an exposed aggregate finish are used to create an interesting labyrinth pattern.*

adjacent limestone wall. The pavement was installed without expansion joints, and the thin limestone veneer was no match for the expanding precast concrete pavers.

Figure 5-3 These high-quality precast concrete bollards approach the appearance of limestone.

Figure 5-4 Appearances suggest that this damage was caused by expansion of the precast pavers against the limestone wall without the benefit of an expansion joint.

Early generations of precast paving and wall systems were rightfully criticized by designers for their overall monochromatic uniformity and appearance. Naturally occurring materials, such as stone or the clay that is used to manufacture bricks, exhibit an organic variation in their hue and tone that imparts a richness and a character that is difficult to manufacture artificially. Fortunately, ongoing research and progress in the coloration of precast systems has given them a higher degree of variegation in color and texture. Tumbling the pavers is one technique that yields a more natural-looking and less precise stone face. Precast manufacturers are increasingly offering product lines in which the individual colors are carefully mixed on every palette. Continued product improvement has significantly enhanced the appearance of segmental paving and walls, raising their acceptance among both designers and their clients.

Another distinct advantage of flexible unit pavers, such as precast, brick, or stone, is the relative ease with which individual units can be removed and replaced. For example, maintenance or repair of an underground utility line that lies beneath asphalt or cast-in-place concrete requires the removal of original, integral material and subsequent patching with a nonintegral replacement material. The patch never quite matches the surrounding material, leaving a permanent "scar." Nor is a patch ever quite as structurally sound as the original homogenous material. It represents a weakened point that is more likely to fail under the stresses of traffic and weather. In contrast, flexible pavers can simply be removed and stockpiled until replacement is called for. The resulting surface performs and appears as seamless as when new, provided the replacement is done properly.

Figure 5-5 Tumbled, split-face precast concrete retaining-wall units do not require mortared joints.

STANDARDS

Segmental precast pavements are nearly always installed as flexible pavement systems. The pavers are laid hand-tight, with no mortar joints. They can be laid over flexible (aggregate) bases or rigid (concrete or asphalt) bases for extra stability. The installation

Figure 5-6 Contrasting precast unit pavers set into a cast-in-place concrete walkway announce the approaching vehicular roadway.

Figure 5-7 The highly consistent dimensions of these precast concrete pavers greatly facilitated the installation of this complex paving pattern.

shown in Figure 5-6 clearly announces the adjacent intersection and enhances the user safety of the pavement. However, if the same precast installation were to settle differentially from the surrounding cast-in-place concrete, the result would be a hazardous condition. The installation shown in the figure is set on a rigid base of concrete and has not settled in

several years. With a rigid base, the overriding issue becomes drainage, as the concrete base and the surrounding concrete curb would trap and hold water if not adequately drained. Joint sand or bedding sand is the best choice for the setting bed of a flexible paving system. As with all flexible systems, an edge restraint is required that is compatible with the dimensions and mass of the unit pavers.

Color in precast concrete is the result of pigments or other colorants added to the concrete mix. Unlike stone and brick, precast manufacturers are not limited to the hues provided by nature alone. Choosing colors for precast units is much like choosing wall colors from paint chips. Designers are advised to select from samples that represent the entire range of color choices and variations. Surface textures and finishes for precast concrete units are as varied as the manufacturers. As with colors, samples are necessary for final selection. Finish textures can be the direct result of the molds used in production, or they can be applied using a number of postmolding processes, such as tumbling or sandblasting.

Figure 5-8 *This grid of precast concrete pavers permits limited vehicular traffic, stabilizes the sandy slope, and permits water to pass through rather than run off the pavement.*

PERMEABLE PRECAST PAVING

The growing emphasis placed on sustainable land development practices makes drainage, water quality, and groundwater recharge high priorities. Large impervious pavements and buildings have the largest impacts on stormwater drainage systems. It follows that very significant improvements can be achieved through the increased use of porous or permeable paving systems.

Figure 5-9 Water permeability and the filtration of contaminants are achieved with precast concrete pavers through the chamfered corners and the resulting voids.

Precast concrete is essentially impervious to water penetration, but that does not mean that pavements composed of precast concrete cannot contribute to a comprehensive program of effective stormwater management. The key to permeable precast paving lies in the design of the *joints,* and creating voids between the pavers rather than in the porosity of the pavers themselves. Flexible paving systems, with their nonmortared joints, have always allowed a certain amount of water to penetrate the pavement surface. Permeable pavements owe their capacity for stormwater drainage to the size and configuration of the joints. The paving grid system shown in Figure 5-8 is suitable for vehicular traffic and provides excellent permeability for drainage. However, its large voids do not adequately support many types of foot traffic, and can be especially challenging for individuals with disabilities.

The precast pavers shown in Figure 5-9 utilize chamfered corners to funnel stormwater into the resulting rectangular voids, and into the base courses and soil beneath. Other systems rely on a series of flanges located on the lateral faces of the pavers to ensure adequate joint spacing between adjacent pavers. These systems can achieve voids in the range of 12 percent of the total surface area. Over a single acre of otherwise impervious pavement, that represents more than 5,200 square feet of pervious surface. To perform optimally, it is recommended that the base course of crushed stone be open graded and rated for rapid drainage. Likewise, the bedding course should be free of fines that can impede water percolation. It should be noted that ASTM C-33, *Concrete and Bedding Sand,* is *not recommended* for filling the voids in permeable paving systems, as these materials do not provide an adequate filtration rate. When properly installed, these permeable systems are effective at filtering heavy metals and other water-borne contaminants, as well as at facilitating groundwater recharge.

SEGMENTAL PRECAST RETAINING WALLS

Segmental precast retaining walls continue to enjoy immense popularity because they offer a number of significant advantages over traditional retaining-wall design. They offer beauty and performance at an economic price. They do not require the deep, reinforced footings necessary for

Figure 5-10 Segmental precast concrete retaining walls require no mortar, are relatively simple to install, and require minimal footings.

cast-in-place concrete retaining walls, nor do they require any formwork. They effectively eliminate the buildup of hydrostatic pressure. Installation is simpler and requires less specialized equipment, and the range of colors and finishes gives designers

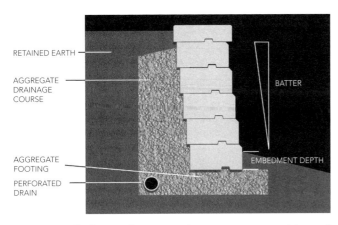

RETAINED EARTH

AGGREGATE DRAINAGE COURSE

BATTER

AGGREGATE FOOTING

PERFORATED DRAIN

EMBEDMENT DEPTH

Figure 5-11 The basics of a segmental precast concrete retaining-wall system. Although the specific configuration will vary somewhat by manufacturer, this demonstrates the simplicity of segmental retaining walls and the importance of drainage in their detailing.

tremendous flexibility in harmonizing with other site elements.

The foundation of a segmental retaining wall is simply a course of aggregate to a depth of a foot or so. It need not be excavated to frost depth. This measure

alone represents a tremendous advantage over deeper cast-in-place concrete footings. Typically, only a single course of wall units is embedded in grade. Provided this course is properly leveled and the base course has been adequately compacted, installation of the remainder of the wall is relatively simple. The precast wall units are not mortared into place, and a system of keys or pins ensures the proper placement of subsequent courses. Each course is set back slightly from the previous course, giving the face a batter that helps to resist overturning and enhances overall stability.

As with any retaining wall, drainage is a critical issue. Perforated footing drains are recommended, as is a vertical drainage course of aggregate behind the wall itself. Weep holes are not necessary, as the individual open joints permit water to migrate through the wall along its entire face.

LEARNING ACTIVITIES

Prepare a plan for a 15-foot × 15-foot patio area using any commercially available precast paving unit, such as Unilock products or similar materials.

1. Use a scale of 1 inch = 1 foot-0 inches.
2. Use at least two colors of pavers to achieve an interesting pattern.
   a. Indicate the manufacturer, paver type, and desired finish.

b. Identify and label the edge restraint system.
c. Indicate the thickness and dimensions of all specified pavers.

CHAPTER **6** **METAL**

GENERAL

The exterior environment places tremendous stress on materials. The more densely populated urban environment is especially demanding. Weather, vehicular traffic, heavy use, pollution, and even vandalism combine to take a toll on landscape construction materials. Metal is a material that is well suited to the most extreme stresses found in the built environment. Metal serves a nearly endless list of functions in the landscape. It is used for manhole covers and drains that must support the heaviest of traffic loads. It is used to construct play equipment in the most intensely used public parks, and provides durable seating that stands up to the challenges of high-demand public landscapes. Metal even protects trees and plantings in sidewalks and pavements.

Historical developments in metallurgy have often accompanied significant advances in the history of humankind. The Iron Age and Bronze Age were eras in which cultures learned the "alchemical" skills necessary to transform raw materials into utilitarian objects with remarkable strength and durability. Tremendous leaps in knowledge and craftsmanship accompanied these discoveries. Even today, many of the most common surnames found in Western countries—including Smith, Schmidt, Herrero, and Kowalski—suggest an ancestor's talent for transforming metal with heat and force. Such was the importance of the metal smith's contributions within a community.

Unlike masonry materials, metal has the distinct advantage of being strong in both compression and tension. It can span while supporting extremely heavy loads, as evidenced by its widespread use in bridge construction. Metal elements such as manhole covers, drain inlets, and gutters are essentially small bridges themselves, which must support vehicular traffic while spanning the void created by a manhole or drain.

CHARACTERISTICS OF METAL

Metal is either elemental or an alloy of metallic elements. Among the metals most commonly used in landscape applications, iron (Fe), copper (Cu), and aluminum (Al) have places on the periodic table of elements. Steel, brass, and bronze are examples of *alloys*, or mixtures, of elements.

Metal is formed or shaped into landscape components in a variety of ways, but most typically these methods involve heat. Cooled metal is strong and durable, but also difficult to work. Some metal can be slowly lathed or ground into shape, but more often metal is heated to a malleable or even a molten state to achieve its final shape and dimensions. Metal can be worked under the hammer, cast into molds, cut from plates, or extruded (as aluminum often is).

There is a long list of optional finishes for metals. Over time, most untreated metal will oxidize to varying degrees—which may be desirable or not. Oxidized

copper weathers over time to a familiar green that is prized for its unique character and color. The oxidation of iron and steel is called *rust*. Rust is an unwelcome guest on our automobiles, but its familiar reddish-orange hues are the targeted outcome of weathering steel, commonly known under its trademarked name, Cor-Ten steel. For metals like aluminum and stainless steel, oxidation is far more subtle. Galvanizing is a common treatment for retarding oxidation when it is undesirable. In contrast, the art of patination can yield a variety of colors and the appearance of graceful age on metal surfaces.

STANDARDS

There are few construction materials that offer the diversity of metal. The technology of metallurgy is the subject of constant research and refinement. Particular emphasis has been placed on making metal stronger and lighter. This has been true from the Iron Age through the Industrial Revolution up to the present. The standards that govern the performance of construction metal must remain current and are under continued review and revision. Some metals, like aluminum and steel, have a significant place in the built landscape, while other metals, like platinum and brass, are less common. Metal is often relied on to perform a load-bearing structural role or to provide needed security in a designed landscape. Public safety and the integrity of the installation are at stake in both cases. Failure to specify metal of the necessary strength, durability, or dimension can be catastrophic.

ASTM International, originally known as the American Society for Testing and Materials, maintains active standards for every metal used in landscape construction. It is incumbent on the landscape designer to become familiar with the content of those standards.

IRON

Iron is a strong, dense metal used for some of the most durable components in the built environment. Iron castings are frequently used where heavy traffic calls for a material that can support a load while spanning a subterranean opening such as a drain or manhole. These include manhole frames and covers, catchbasin frames and grates, gutter inlets, and a wide variety of drainage grates. Tree grates in paved areas are

Figure 6-1 A cast-iron trench drain.

Figure 6-2 This cast-iron tree grate supports intense urban traffic while permitting water to reach some of the tree's roots. When selecting tree grates, consider expandability as the tree's caliper grows. This tree grate allows the option of installing up-lighting.

Figure 6-3 Wrought iron is the result of a skilled blacksmith artfully working heated iron into desired shapes. Many components that appear to be wrought iron are actually formed by casting molten iron into molds.

another familiar use of cast iron. *Cast* iron, as its name suggests, is cast into a mold while it is in a molten state, then allowed to cool.

Wrought iron recalls the days of the village blacksmith, a craftworker who heated, bent, and

shaped iron with a hammer over an anvil until a specific, desired shape was achieved. True wrought iron and the craftsmanship needed to produce it are rare today, with most coming from small, boutique shops.

Products marketed as wrought iron are more commonly mild steel, which maintains the historic look and feel of wrought iron.

STEEL

Steel is used in an enormous variety of landscape applications. It is useful for seating and benches, handrails, railings, and bollards. Steel rebar lends its tensile strength to the compressive strength of concrete.

Steel is an alloy, not an element. Its primary component is iron, which is alloyed with carbon. The increased carbon content makes steel both harder and stronger than iron. A variety of modern steels are manufactured today. The most common is A36 steel, the structural steel found in the load-carrying members of most large structures. Steel-frame construction gave birth to the modern skyscraper, replacing structural stone as the most reliable way to build vertically.

Various alloys of steel are defined by their components. Stainless steel must contain at least

Figure 6-4 *A graceful yet strong and stable steel rail safely permits a close encounter with nature.*

10½ percent chromium. It is much more resistant to oxidation and corrosion than standard steel. It is also more costly than standard steel. Another steel alloy, called *weathering* steel, was formulated to provide a stable and attractive oxidized finish that eliminated the need for painting. The patina

Figure 6-5 With high-gloss painted finishes, steel site furnishings are both durable and visually attractive.

Figure 6-6 The carefully considered detailing of a steel rail allows it to enhance the overall design of a public open space.

process ages the surface of the steel to a rich, warm reddish-brown. Cor-Ten, although it is a trademarked name for a brand of weathering steel, has become an interchangeable term for the product itself.

Steel is simple and economical to recycle and is the most commonly recycled metal in North America. Recycled steel loses none of its strength or hardness during recycling and is far cheaper to produce than the "virgin" steel created by the process of extracting iron ore and refining it.

Galvanizing

One of the notable drawbacks of ferrous metals such as iron and steel is their propensity to corrode, or rust. The harsh exterior climate promotes the corrosion and oxidation of steel. Corroded steel fasteners used in exterior wood carpentry will result in unattractive staining. Far worse, they will ultimately lose their structural integrity and will fail. Galvanizing is an effective method for treating the surface of ferrous metals to prevent or significantly retard corrosion.

Galvanizing refers to the process of plating the surface of metal with a coating of zinc, an elemental metal that is highly resistant to corrosion. Metal is submerged in a solution of 98 percent pure molten

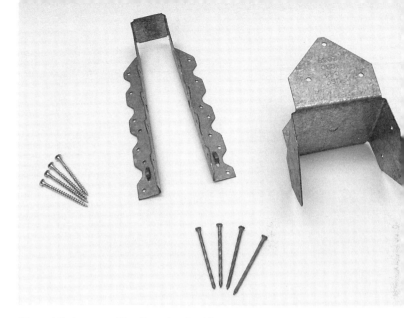

Figure 6-7 *An array of familiar galvanized fasteners.*

zinc at a temperature of 850°F. The result is a long-lasting physical barrier against the elements. Steel used to fabricate exterior fasteners (nails, screws, bolts, etc.) and for a variety of exterior brackets (joist hangers, post anchors, ties, connectors, etc.) is typically galvanized.

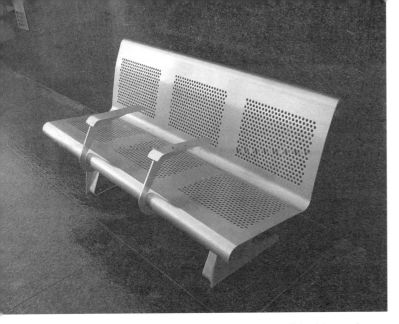

Figure 6-8 *Aluminum is a corrosion-resistant and durable metal suitable for urban environments.*

Figure 6-9 *These innovative aluminum benches are integral components that reinforce the design concept of discovery for this research facility.*

ALUMINUM

Aluminum, *Al* on the periodic table, is one of the most abundant metals on earth, but it is paradoxically extremely rare in its pure form. In nature aluminum is found in combination with hundreds of other minerals.

Like gold and copper, aluminum is very ductile—that is, it can sustain significant deformation without fracture. It is valued in landscape applications because it is highly resistant to corrosion. Aluminum demonstrates a surprising strength compared to its relatively light weight.

We encounter aluminum in every aspect of our lives, from automobiles to packaging to electronics. In landscape design, aluminum is used for a wide variety of site furnishings, including benches, bollards, flagpoles, and gratings. The precise finish and hue of an aluminum surface can range from silvery and reflective to a matte gray, depending on the smoothness of the finished surface. Highly polished aluminum is among the most reflective metal surfaces available.

Aluminum can be shaped using a variety of methods, including stamping, casting, machining, and extruding. Aluminum is easily recycled, and aluminum beverage cans are the single most frequently recycled consumer item.

BRONZE

Bronze is a visually rich metal with a long history of enhancing the built environment. Bronze has historically been a favored metal for casting exterior sculptures. In the landscape it can be used in place of iron castings for elements such as tree grates, trench drains, drain covers, manhole covers, and even bollards, lightposts, and fixtures. The beauty, strength, and durability of bronze do not come without a cost, though; bronze

Figure 6-10 A whimsical bronze casting that serves both as play equipment and as a distinctive design element.

castings are at the upper end of the price range for landscape elements.

Bronze is an alloy, the principal element of which is copper. Bronze can be composed of a variety of other elements, but tin is the most commonly used.

Figures 6-11 and 6-12 These bronze drainage grates beautifully express the marriage of aesthetics and function.

Aluminum, silicon, and manganese can also combine with copper to create bronze alloys. Like copper, only the surface of bronze oxidizes, forming a protective barrier that resists further oxidation; therefore, bronze excels at withstanding the stresses of the exterior environment. The oxidation of bronze results in one of the most admired patinas of any metal.

METAL FASTENERS AND REINFORCEMENTS

Because of its durability and strength, metal is often called upon to play an invisible supporting role in landscape applications. Reinforcing bar adds strength to cast-in-place concrete. Nails, screws, and bolts secure

Figure 6-13 *Fasteners must be strong and reliable. Fastener failure can be costly and even catastrophic.*

Figure 6-14 *Though among the simplest of fasteners, not all nails are suitable for exterior landscape applications.*

wood components together, and metal ties unify brick and concrete block into an integral whole.

Nails

The simplest metal fasteners are probably nails. A nail is composed of three simple parts: a head, a shank, and a point. Nails are driven into wood using either manual hammers or power nailers. Because softwoods are most commonly used in landscape construction, predrilling is not typically necessary as it is with hardwoods such as oak, cherry, or maple. Despite a nail's utter simplicity, there are distinct characteristics that set nails meant for outdoor use apart from their interior cousins.

Exterior nails should be either galvanized (the most common and affordable option) or stainless steel, to inhibit rusting. The shank should not be smooth, as it is with common nails. Smooth-shank nails are prone to backing out, an especially vexing problem with horizontal exterior decking that can result in dangerously exposed nail heads. Ring shanks or spiral shanks help prevent nails from backing out due to movement from traffic or freeze-and-thaw cycles. Exterior nails often sport a wide head embossed with a fine grid of dimpling called a "checkered roof." This textured surface complements the checkered face of

a framing hammer to minimize occurrences where the hammer glances off the nail head during installation. In contrast, the proportionally small heads of finish nails stand little chance of permanently fastening exterior softwoods.

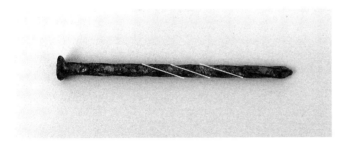

Figure 6-15 The spiral shank of this nail helps it resist backing out of wood components such as exterior decking.

Figure 6-16 The grid, or "checkered roof," on the head of this nail facilitates installation in wood construction.

Nails are sized using an antiquated system in which the base unit is the "penny" or "pence." Abbreviated "d," the numerical value represents the cost in pence of 100 nails, *at some point in the distant past.* Because larger nails cost more than smaller nails, larger penny units represent larger nails. There was a time in history when 100 nails of a specific size cost 8 pence, or pennies. Even though the costs have risen over the centuries, these nails are still referred to as 8 penny, or 8d, nails, and are incrementally larger than 6d nails and smaller than 10d nails. The stout nails needed to fasten dimensional exterior lumber often fall into the 8d to 12d size range.

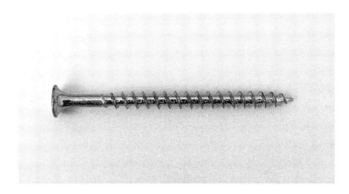

Figure 6-17 *Screws take more time to install than nails, but provide greater holding power with far less tendency to back out of exterior softwoods. Bugle-head deck screws are specifically designed for attaching decking to joists.*

Screws

Exterior screws are superior to nails for securing softwoods, but are also costlier and more time-consuming to install. Simply defined, a *screw* is a spirally threaded metal fastener, usually (but not in all cases) with a tapered point. Its razor-sharp threads cut into the wood itself and are not matched with another fastener as with a nut-and-bolt arrangement. Like nails, screws have heads. The head of a screw is configured to match a driver that rotationally pushes the screw into wood. The familiar Phillips head is the most commonly used in exterior construction because of the relative ease of insertion and ability to use a power screwdriver. It is far more cumbersome to align a driver in a straight slotted-head screw than in a Phillips head. Square-drive heads are also popular for exterior construction.

As with nails, screws must also resist corrosion via galvanizing or stainless steel manufacture. Exterior screws typically have threads that are razor-sharp, flare wider, and are spaced further apart than common screws. Each of these features enhance the screw's ability to grip and hold soft woods. Low-profile threads that are tightly spaced would be far more prone to stripping the hole and losing their grip on the wood.

Exterior screws, especially deck screws, often have a bugle-shaped radius where the head meets the shank. This gradual flaring works much like a brake, slowing the force of power screwdrivers and preventing the screw from becoming buried too deeply in soft wood. The bugle-head shape facilitates driving the screw to the desired depth, helping the installer to maintain the speed and economy afforded by power tools.

Screws are sized by a reference number that indicates their diameter, their length in inches, their head configuration, their finish, and their thread type. A typical deck screw might be specified as "#8 x 2½ deck screw, Phillips drive, bugle head, galvanized, coarse thread, exterior use." In this example,

"#8" refers to the diameter of the screw. To convert this to inches, use the following formula:

Screw diameter (in inches) = ((screw# 13) + 60)/1000

So, using our previous example:

#8 screw diameter = ((8 13) + 60)/1000 = 0.164 inch

Nuts and Bolts

The nut-and-bolt configuration represents the strongest method of fastening two or more wood elements together. Like screws, bolts are threaded. Unlike screws, though, the threads of a bolt are precisely machined to match a nut rather than to dig into the wood itself. A properly sized nut-and-bolt connection is virtually indestructible and will long outlive the wood components it binds.

Like nails and screws, a bolt is a headed fastener. Bolts are not tapered, and have an exacting thread specification that accepts a nontapered nut. Because of this precise threading, threads-per-inch is a key component in specifying bolts.

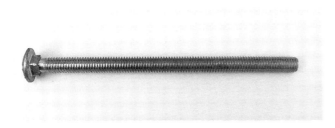

Figure 6-18 Bolts, combined with washers and nuts, provide outstanding fastening of wood components. This carriage bolt has a user-friendly rounded head.

Bolts feature a variety of head shapes, the most common being the hex head, which is driven by a wrench. As with hammers and screwdrivers, wrenches can be manual or power-driven. Other head configurations are square head, rounded, and carriage head. A *carriage head* is a smooth, human-friendly head that cannot be turned with a wrench. Rather, the nut must be tightened. To facilitate tightening, carriage bolts usually have a squared "shoulder" just beneath the head to prevent the bolt from spinning in its hole during tightening.

Hex-head bolts are decidedly less human friendly. To minimize the chance of an unwelcome encounter, hex-head bolts should be countersunk wherever contact is possible. *Countersinking* refers to the practice of drilling of a second hole that is both wide and deep enough to accept the entire head of a bolt without it standing proud of (protruding from) the finished surface of the wood.

The sheer strength of a nut-and-bolt fastener can damage softwoods by excessively compressing the wood cells during tightening. Broad washers at both the head and the nut location help to spread out the compressive force of the fastener and to minimize unwanted deflection of the wood surface. Some washers intended for exterior construction are configured with small teeth that grip the face of the wood and inhibit spinning during installation.

There are instances in which the strength of a bolt is required, but the end of the bolt is not accessible for attaching and tightening the nut. One such case is attaching the ledger board of a deck system to the framing of a house or building. In this instance, a

Figure 6-19 Rebar serves to strengthen and reinforce cast-in-place concrete.

fastener called a *lag bolt* is most often called for. Lag bolts are misnamed. They are tapered and do not match with a nut; rather, they dig into the surrounding wood of the structural framing, so technically they are screws. But traditions in the building trades are typically

difficult to change (take the "penny" designation of nails as an example!), so be prepared to specify this fastener as a bolt and not as the screw it truly is.

Reinforcing Bar

Reinforcing bar, also known as *rebar* or *rerod,* is not technically a fastener, although it often serves to span between two adjacent elements, such as adjoining slabs of cast-in-place concrete. As its name suggests, rebar *reinforces* another material. In concrete, it complements that material's compressive strength with its own inherent tensile strength. Rebar is ribbed steel that is available in different diameters. The ribbing firmly secures the rebar in cured concrete. Common applications in the landscape include cast-in-place walls, steps, bollards, and any exterior foundations needed for arbors, gazebos, or shelters.

Rebar is used to maintain vertical alignment between adjacent slabs of concrete pavement, or where concrete pavement meets concrete steps. In these cases, differential settling or movement could result in a hazardous situation. The rebar does not prevent vertical displacement, but it dictates that the adjoining elements will move together, maintaining an even (and safe) transition between them. When using rebar for this purpose, care must be taken to allow for horizontal expansion. The ribbed surface of rebar is designed specifically to bond with the surrounding concrete, naturally impeding its expansion. One of the two ends of rebar must be wrapped or treated with a bond-breaker or lubricant to allow for horizontal movement while maintaining vertical alignment.

Like screws, the diameter of rebar is sized using a reference number. However, although the nomenclature appears similar, the math behind the sizing of rebar is entirely different. The number followed by the pound symbol (#) indicates the bar diameter in eighths of an inch. Thus, #4 rebar (a size of rebar commonly used in landscape construction) is four-eighths of an inch, or ½ inch in diameter.

When rebar is incorporated into cast-in-place concrete, it is important to maintain complete encapsulation of the rebar. When even a small surface area of rebar is exposed to the elements, it is likely to rust. Steel expands when it oxidizes, and the force of the expansion can crack the surrounding concrete. Construction details should call for a minimum of 1 inch of "clear cover" of concrete surrounding all steel reinforcing bars or woven-wire fabric placed within the concrete.

Metal-Wire Mesh

Flexible metal mesh plays a unique role in landscape construction. Easily bent by hand, it would seem to offer little in the way of serious reinforcement. When configured into a tough, unified grid, though, metal wire performs a remarkable job of integrating elements, much the way that flimsy drywall tape works to strengthen drywall joints.

Two common examples of wire meshing used in the landscape are woven-wire fabric and brick/masonry ties. Their primary role is to unify masonry elements into a more integral whole. Woven-wire fabric (WWF), also known as woven-wire mesh (WWM), is commonly called for as an element in cast-in-place concrete pavements. Woven-wire fabric does not prevent cracking, but it serves as a matrix to hold concrete together when the inevitable cracking does occur. When a crack occurs in unreinforced concrete, the result is two entirely disconnected masses of concrete. The matrix of the

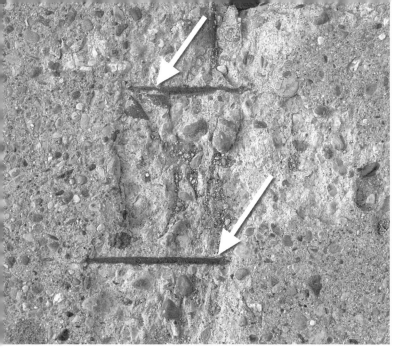

Figure 6-20 *Failure reveals the woven-wire mesh originally installed in this concrete walkway. A minimum of 1 inch of concrete should envelop all woven-wire mesh. It is likely that this mesh was set too shallow, contributing to this failure.*

metal grid, when embedded integrally into the slab, works to hold the concrete masses together and inhibits further movement and separation.

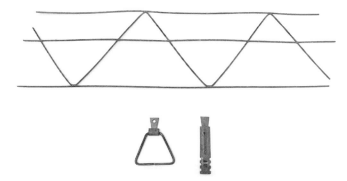

Figure 6-21 *Don't forget to specify the brick ties! These invisible but important fasteners integrate horizontal brick courses with the structural backup material of block or cast-in-place concrete. The ties on the top work with concrete masonry units and the ties on the bottom fit into a matching channel set into cast-in-place concrete.*

A typical specification for woven-wire fabric denotes both the size of the metal wire to be used and the spacing of the wire grid. "6 x 6, 10/10 WWF" indicates that the grid is to be spaced six inches apart in both directions, using #10 wire, also in both directions.

Masonry ties appear as unsubstantial as does woven-wire fabric—yet their task is no less than to secure several tons of brick or stone to a backup material composed of several tons of concrete masonry units while spanning a void of some 2 inches. Just as with woven-wire mesh, the strength of masonry ties is derived from their configuration into a meshlike form. When embedded into the horizontal mortar joints of every sixth course of brick and every other course of concrete block, the bond between the two materials is substantial. Without masonry ties, the wall is very likely to fail (and the landscape designer is likely to get sued!).

LEARNING ACTIVITIES

Chart out a walking route approximately one mile in length on or near your campus.

1. Find and catalog all of the landscape applications that are entirely or primarily composed of metal.
2. To the best of your ability, identify what metallic element or alloy is used in each item.
3. To the best of your ability, identify how the metal surface is finished.
4. Identify the manufacturer of at least one of the metal items you catalogued on your walk. Locate this manufacture's Website, then locate and print the specific catalogue cut and/or specification for this product.

GENERAL

At the upper end of the price range, stone has earned a unique niche in the built environment. It represents quality, durability, and permanence. It also suggests luxury. Stone is available in an enormous array of colors, finishes, and textures. Long before humans developed the knowledge and skill to make brick or concrete, stone was readily available to be gathered and assembled as a strong and durable building material.

One of the characteristics of stone that is most valued by design professionals is its aura of permanence and authenticity. It is neither synthetic nor easily reproduced. It took nature and natural processes tens of thousands of years to create the rich and beautiful stone that we so greatly admire today. Some stone dates back to the formation of the earth itself. Furthermore, stone beautifully reflects those geological formative processes. Its colors, patterns, grains, and textures convey the tortuous violence of volcanoes, the

Figure 7-1 In the hands of an artist or a skilled stone mason, stone can be made into high-quality and long-lasting artifacts in the landscape.

Figure 7-2 Since ancient times, stone in its purest form has been simply gathered and stacked to form durable walls and structures.

immense power of glaciers, the collision of tectonic plates, and the unrelenting force of water.

Stone is essentially a gift of nature. Stone masons do not manufacture stone. Rather, they have developed a long-standing tradition of revealing stone and transforming it into building components of great beauty and utility. Stone workers, sculptors, and landscape designers all share a deeply held respect for stone. Within the rich tradition of Japanese gardens, stone placement and grouping has been elevated to a venerated art form. Many of the most profound expressions of art and architecture, in the East or the West, are conveyed in the medium of stone.

Among the more rewarding activities of a career in landscape design is the opportunity to leave the office to spend time in the field. This may involve visiting a construction site or tagging plant materials for a specific project at their source. Very high on the list is a visit to the local stone supplier to inspect and select material for a project. Selecting stone from catalog cuts or online images is not advisable. You can appreciate stone fully only when you can see it in natural exterior light and get a feel for its texture, hue, and general character. A knowledgeable designer knows which varieties of stone are available locally and will nurture a working relationship with those suppliers who provide stone and the other components necessary for landscape-making.

Figure 7-3 A visit to the stoneyard is an exceptional treat for land-scape designers. It is important to become familiar with the types and characteristics of stone available locally and regionally.

GEOLOGY 101

It is not necessary for landscape designers to become expert geologists in order to employ the beauty and merits of stone in their designs. Nevertheless, it is useful to know how stone came to be, and how its formation translates into its diverse physical properties, including strength, water resistance, and workability. Just as carpenters approach working with pine and oak in very different ways, it is critical for landscape designers to understand the *fundamental* differences between stone as diverse as limestone and granite. Both are stone, but the similarities end there. Understanding the natural processes that gave birth to a particular type of stone will aid tremendously in using it properly in outdoor environments.

All terrestrial stone began life as something else. The natural processes that lead to the creation of stone are varied and complex. There are three broad categories of stone, and each has a place in the built landscape. Geologists categorize stone as sedimentary, igneous, or metamorphic.

Sedimentary Stone

As its name suggests, *sedimentary* stone results from the buildup of sediments that accumulate and become consolidated and cemented together over time. The various sedimentary stones are classified according to the nature and source of their constituent sediments. The composition and strength of sedimentary stone can be quite diverse, depending on the types of sediment from which it originated and the specific mineralogy of the cement. Clay sediments develop into shale. Sand sediments yield sandstone. Limestone most often derives from sediments composed of marine and lake organisms whose shells and structure are largely calcite, though not all limestone is organic in origin.

Sedimentary stone is not further hardened by pressure or transformed by heat, and its varieties are among the softest of stones. The relative softness of sedimentary stone creates a greater likelihood of staining and discoloration compared to other types of stone. Sedimentary stone has a greater capacity to absorb water, along with impurities, than harder stones. It can also discolor under prolonged exposure to pollution and acid rain.

Metamorphic Stone

The word *metamorphosis* means "to change form," to transform from one thing into another. In the creation of metamorphic stone, heat and pressure combine to alter a parent material into a harder and denser internal structure. That parent material, called the *protolith*, can be any of the three types of stone. Slate, and to a lesser degree marble, are the metamorphic stones that landscape designers encounter most frequently. The protolith of slate is shale, a sedimentary stone. Heat and pressure work their magic on another sedimentary stone, limestone, to yield marble.

Igneous Stone

The word *igneous* hints at heat and fire. It shares the same root as the word *ignite*, which means "to set afire." Igneous rocks are in fact the result of cooling magma . . . rock so intensely heated that it has become liquefied or molten. Igneous rocks include some of the densest, hardest, and most water resistant rocks on earth. Geologists have identified and classified an enormous variety of igneous rocks, but the most useful in landscape applications is granite. Basalt, prized for its black or dark-gray coloration, is also employed in exterior pavements, but in significantly smaller quantities than granite. The exceptional qualities of granite and basalt do not come without a price. These are also among the costliest hardscape options available.

CHARACTERISTICS OF STONE

Like most masonry materials, stone is at its best when placed under compressive rather than tensile stresses. That is to say that stone, while being very strong and durable, is also relatively brittle. Any stone proposed to be used in a spanning, unsupported configuration must be carefully evaluated for its structural load-bearing capabilities. Stone placed on a well-designed base of compacted aggregate and earth is nearly indestructible.

Stone is a naturally occurring material. Its "factory" is nature and the various forces exerted upon the stone to give it its unique physical characteristics. As such, there is always a degree of variability in stone. Compressive strength is among those variables. A specific stone's psi (pounds per square inch) strength is given as a *minimum,* not an average. Thus, the majority of a specified stone delivered to the jobsite will possess

Figure 7-4 *While retaining its naturalistic qualities, stone has been shaped and carefully fitted to create this graceful yet substantial retaining wall.*

higher compressive values than the reported minimum. Its precise composition may vary across its mass as well, and relatively weak cleavage planes occur in many kinds of stone.

Figure 7-5 Two millennia after its installation, hand-crafted stonework and masonry are durable reminders of the original structures and the hands that created them.

Stone often has a grain. In nature, the grain of sedimentary stone is typically horizontal, reflecting the accumulative process of its formation. The grain of igneous stones displays the remarkable flow of molten material, giving witness to its birth millennia ago. Grain orientation often plays a role in design. Building stone that is set with its grain oriented according to its original direction (usually horizontal) is said to be on its "natural bed." When the grain of a stone is oriented perpendicular to its origin (usually vertical), it is said to be "on edge." Stone placed on its natural bed might yield a sense of repose, relaxation, and order, whereas stone set on edge can create interest, contrast, or even tension.

Building stone is quarried, not manufactured. In order to acquire building stone, the earth must be disturbed by human industry. Supplies of all natural resources, including stone, are finite. Even the most productive quarry will eventually be exhausted, necessitating the reclamation and healing of the disturbed landscape. Humankind's thirst for stone has resulted in an industry that has succeeded for millennia in accomplishing what would seem nearly unthinkable: the successful extraction of huge blocks of stone cleaved neatly from the earth. The astonishing stone constructions of the Egyptians, the Romans, and the Renaissance cathedral builders continue to inspire awe, wonder, and even debate regarding their precise methods of construction and engineering. Necessity *is* the mother of invention, but it was not the necessity for stone that drove these ambitious masonry undertakings; it was more the *desire* to build with it. As a building material, stone has always represented luxury. Its use in a building or monument conveys a message of importance and status . . . even immortality. Peasants built with modest, short-lived materials, while the nobility built with stone.

This text often refers to particular materials as *authentic*. Stone certainly qualifies for this adjective. Still, *authentic* is an admittedly subjective term that requires some parameters. It suggests the opposite of artificial. Authentic materials do not degrade or decay with age; rather, they improve under the combined forces of age, weather, and human activity, acquiring a rich patina in the process. Authenticity suggests longevity and grace. It also implies richness and depth. Stone is stone to its very core.

Figure 7-6 *A sedimentary stone, limestone is an outstanding choice for carved and shaped landscape details.*

STONE: STONE BY STONE

Limestone

Limestone is a sedimentary stone. Its minimal compressive strength is similar to that of concrete, typically around 4,000 psi. Some limestone, such as Indiana limestone, is extremely consistent in composition, texture, color, and density, whereas other types of limestone vary across their mass, yielding more mottled tones and a wider range of colors. The consistency of Indiana limestone gives it a high degree of machinability. It is excellent for use in creating landscape details and ornamentation. Other varieties of limestone range in color from dark gray to mottled gold to red. Because limestone is frequently composed of shell and shell fragments, some of the more unique varieties prominently feature intact remnants of shells in their composition. Designers should take note that not all limestone is suitable for the extremes of exterior use.

Among the many options available to designers, limestone may not be the ideal choice for a paving material. It is less dense than metamorphic or igneous stone and it has a greater capacity to absorb water. The groundwater beneath a pavement is rarely free of soil constituents, which are carried to the surface of the limestone by capillary action. This will eventually lead to noticeable staining and discoloration. If limestone is proposed to be used as a pavement where staining would be objectionable, it is advisable to seal its underside with a waterproofing agent that is specifically recommended for this use.

Limestone is among the best materials available for details and ornamentation. Its relative softness makes it is easy to machine, yielding crisp and precise surfaces and lines when worked by a qualified stone mason. Limestone carvers are very much like carpenters in the manner and techniques they employ to work the stone. The partnership between the landscape designer and the stone carver is critical. Craftworkers rely upon the knowledgeable and creative designer to best utilize their talents to achieve the true potential of stone. Designers should not underestimate the talents of stone masons; good ones can successfully bring almost any working drawing into three-dimensional reality.

Travertine

Travertine is a unique type of sedimentary stone that is a close relative of limestone. It typically forms near hot, mineral-rich springs. Gas bubbles become trapped, imparting a distinctly textured and pitted surface to the stone. Travertine is available in a wide range of colors, from beige to yellow to rose to red. It is also among the few natural stones that provide designers with a distinctive white option, useful for creating contrast with dark adjacent materials.

Domestic sources of travertine are scarce. The majority is imported from European quarries found in

Figure 7-7 Travertine offers a distinctly white paving option.

Turkey and the well-known deposits at Tivoli, Italy. More recent competition has arisen from quarries in Mexico and Peru.

Sandstone

Sandstone, like limestone, belongs to the family of sedimentary stones, laid down in horizontal strata

Figure 7-8 Few paving patterns are as widely recognized and admired as the intricate design that graces the Piazza Campidoglio in Rome.

Figure 7-9 Like its sedimentary cousin limestone, sandstone is a relatively soft stone that is well suited to the creation of intricate landscape details.

in ancient water bodies. Sandstone is composed of sand-sized grains cemented together by clay, silica, carbonate, or iron oxide. Many of the so-called brownstones (attached row houses) of the nineteenth

century employed sandstone in their facades, giving rise to their name. The rich hues and variety among sandstone deposits keep it in high demand for landscape design.

Flagstone

Perhaps the most common use of sandstone is for flagstone pavers. The term *flagstone* is often applied to any flat, cleaved, and irregularly shaped paver. Technically speaking, though, a flagstone is a flat, irregularly shaped or rectangular (dimensional) paving stone composed of sandstone.

Flagstone comes in a vast array of colors. For landscape designers, a visit to the local or regional stone supplier is like a child's visit to the candy store. Each choice has its own appeal, and decisions are difficult. Installations of flagstone pavement can be either rigid (with mortared joints) or flexible. A particularly appealing visual effect can be achieved when the joints between individual (nonmortared) pavers are dressed with a carefully selected stone aggregate.

Figure 7-10 *The familiar irregular shapes of sandstone flags, or flag-stone, remain a popular choice for informal walks and pavements.*

Bluestone

One variety of sandstone, bluestone, occupies a special niche in the built landscape. As its name suggests, *bluestone* is a fine-grained type of sandstone that nature often—but not always—endowed with extremely desirable bluish to greenish hues. However, not all bluestone falls into this spectrum. Its wide range of hues includes soft lavender, ochre, gray, and tan. In North America,

Figure 7-11 *Bluestone is a regional type of sandstone notable for its unique color range.*

bluestone is quarried primarily in Pennsylvania and New York. Designers might also hear bluestone referred to as "Pennsylvania river rock."

Bluestone is coveted by landscape designers for pavements such as patios and walkways. Finishes include sawn, split-face, cleft, flamed, and tumbled. Bluestone is also well adapted to carving for unique landscape details.

Slate

Slate is a high-quality, fine-grained stone in the metamorphic family. Its protolith is shale. Slate is well known for its *foliated* structure, that is, the pronounced cleavage planes that run horizontally through its structure. The resulting thin, smooth sheets of slate have many landscape applications. It is at its best in the landscape when used in walls, copings, and pavements. Its range of rich, natural colors includes black, blue, green, gray, purple, and even reds. The density and fine grain of slate give it excellent water and ice resistance. Just as Indiana is known for high-quality limestone, Vermont is renowned for its slate quarries.

Designers do not enjoy the same freedom of design with slate that they do with more workable stone such as limestone. Its platelike characteristic is a given, so its applications are limited to uses where thin horizontal units are appropriate. Slate has long been used for blackboards, billiard tables, and roofing tiles, because of its stable horizontal characteristics.

Slate has a number of applications in landscape design, including patios, walkways, and terraces. Slate unit pavers are available in a variety of shapes, including squares, rectangles, and irregular polygons. The minimum recommended thickness for slate pavers is ¾ inch. Different varieties of slate weather at different rates. Highly stable slate will maintain its hue indefinitely and is referred to as "unfading" stone. Other categories are designated as "weathering" or "semiweathering." Weathering shifts the visual appearance of slate toward a brownish hue over time. The weathering of slate is a visual characteristic only and does not measurably affect its structural integrity.

A dense metamorphic stone, slate is naturally resistant to soil-borne impurities and acid, so it makes an ideal paving stone. Its natural cleft provides a degree of slip resistance in wet and icy locations. Nevertheless, not all slate is recommended for exterior use, so designers are advised to consult with suppliers before making a final selection.

Granite

Granite is an igneous stone that began forming when the earth itself was cooling. It is among the hardest of stones, rivaling diamond. As with diamonds, it is the extreme pressure under which granite was formed that gives it such hardness and density. Granite has yet another trait in common with diamonds, and that is its prized crystalline structure. Although many varieties of granite exist, they all have three minerals in common, in varying proportions: All granite is composed of feldspar, quartz, and smaller amounts of mica. Small proportions of other minerals, such as hematite and pyrite, are also present in various types of granite. It is the precise proportions and combinations of these minerals that yield the wide range of color found in granite.

There is evidence that granite has been quarried for at least 6,000 years. Deposits of granite, though

Figure 7-12 *These twin massive slabs of granite provide a one-of-a-kind pedestrian bridge.*

extraordinarily consistent in color and texture, are not without variation, or *variegation*. It is precisely this variegation and movement of grain that distinguish naturally occurring stone from even more consistent synthetic stone. Granite is found on every continent on

Figure 7-13 Small granite units, or "sets," offer designers the strength of granite with a finer grain and texture.

the planet. Although exotic granites from overseas certainly increase a designer's choices, there is no shortage of high-quality domestic granites offering a rich range of hues and textures.

Though costly in comparison to other landscape construction materials, granite excels in the harsh exterior environment. It is nearly impervious to weathering, pollution, and freeze/thaw cycles. Because of its density, granite is notably less porous than other landscape masonry materials. Water absorption is typically 0.2 percent or less, compared with up to 8 percent for paving bricks. The compressive strength of granite is no less impressive: average compressive strengths range from 15,000 to more than 30,000 pounds per square inch. Another advantage imparted to granite by its density is its resistance to expansion and contraction, which is considered insignificant for landscape installations.

Although granite is available in a range of finishes, designers must take care to call for a finish that provides adequate slip resistance for exterior pavements, ramps, and stair treads. A thermal finish, also called a *flame* finish, imparts a suitably rough texture to the paver's walking surface for safe traction, especially when wet. To create a thermal finish, a high-temperature flame and cool water are applied jointly to the granite's surface, causing its internal crystalline structure to fracture and exfoliate. Designers need to examine any supplier's samples of specified granite with the thermal finish

Figure 7-14 Time, traffic, and weathering only enhance the character and patina of beautifully aged granite cobblestones.

Figure 7-15 Granite cobblestones with approximately the same dimensions as brick offer the same flexibility of pattern.

applied, as this finish noticeably mutes the hues of the stone.

For vertical applications of granite, designers enjoy much more freedom of choice. The three basic finishes for granite are thermal, honed, and polished. A honed finish creates a smooth yet

Figure 7-16 Three colors of precisely cut granite pavers create a repeating pattern and complement the surrounding architecture of this intensely used urban plaza.

subtle matte appearance; a polished finish imparts a lustrous appearance that noticeably deepens the stone's color, much like a stone that is wet. A thermal finish is textured and rough to the touch. Other finishes, both standard and custom, can be

achieved through a variety of tools and methods, each imparting its own texture or pattern to the stone. These include sawn, diamond, rubbed and sanded, split-face, and pointed. Each has its own slip resistance qualities and unique visual appearance.

STONE PAVING PATTERNS

Unlike many other landscape construction materials, stone is not rigidly dependent on the need for modularity, which represents a critical economy for materials like brick, precast unit pavers, and lumber. Designers enjoy tremendous freedom to configure their own innovative patterns and layouts. Still, there are tried-and-true patterns that have withstood the test of time and remain popular. Some patterns lend themselves best to flagstone, whereas others require the precision of cut stone. Still others call for smaller units, such as cobblestones. The following figures show a number of stone paving patterns that have enjoyed continued popularity among designers.

Figure 7-17a Irregular, nonfitted.

Figure 7-17b Irregular, fitted.

Figure 7-17c Semi-irregular.

Figure 7-17d Random rectangular.

Figure 7-17e Rectangular.

Figure 7-17f Ashlar.

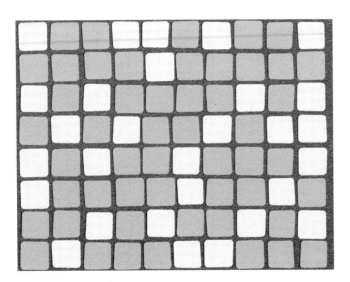

Figure 7-17g Cobblestones.

Figure 7-17h Fishscale.

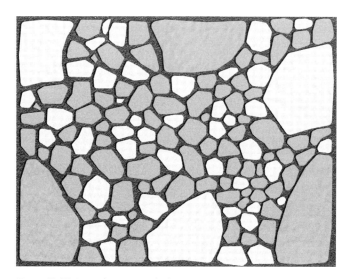

Figure 7-17i Irregular, nongraded.

SYNTHETIC STONE

Synthetic stone is not actually stone at all, but it is more practical and convenient to discuss it in context with authentic stone than elsewhere. As a landscape material, stone is coveted—and it is also expensive. It should come as no surprise that synthetic materials resembling stone, but costing much less, would be developed for the market. It is the prerogative of the individual designer to determine the suitability of synthetic stone (or synthetic anything for that matter) for a specific project, site, client, program, and budget. Although synthetic material can convincingly mimic the visual appearance of its genuine counterpart, it may be limited in other key characteristics. Designers prize stone not only for its appearance on the day a project is completed, but also for the way it matures gracefully, taking on the rich patina of age over many years. Likewise, the naturally occurring variegation of real stone is difficult to simulate artificially. Strength, durability, and density are traits not guaranteed by visual resemblance alone, although some synthetic materials (such as reconstituted granite) can achieve similar specifications.

Conscientious designers must always weigh the overall sustainability of a material before making a final judgment regarding its merit. Rather than dismissing artificial construction materials out of hand, designers must take into consideration the impacts associated with its acquisition, manufacture, transportation, installation, life-cycle longevity, and reuse. Artificial materials that offer significant improvement over natural materials on these criteria are due serious consideration.

Cultured Stone

Cultured stone is essentially a precast Portland cement product. Because it can be mixed with commonly available ingredients and cast into a mold, it achieves significant savings over the quarrying and cutting of real stone. Modern finishing methods do a convincing job of simulating the color and texture of real stone. Cultured stone can be used in pavements as well as in vertical applications. As a wall veneer, it is easier to install than stone, especially when specialized components such as corner units and caps are provided by the manufacturers.

Reconstituted Stone

Unlike cultured stone, reconstituted stone is composed of actual stone. The process of manufacturing reconstituted stone involves forming small particles of stone waste, such as granite. Unit pavers or tiles that are formed under intense pressure demonstrate structural characteristics similar to those of their parent material. Economy is gained by eliminating the need to cut and finish large blocks of stone into the desired final dimensions. The finished units offer designers many of the desirable characteristics of natural stone, but often lack its naturally occurring variegation.

LEARNING ACTIVITIES

1. Select a stone paving pattern presented in this chapter.
   a. Prepare and label a construction detail that clearly communicates your desired pattern to a potential contractor or installer. Use a scale of 1 inch = 1 foot-0 inches.

2. Assume that you have prepared a site plan calling for granite steps and bluestone pavers.

   a. Research and identify one or more suppliers, regionally located if possible, who are capable of providing the stone needed for your project.

   b. Prepare a brief summary of each of these suppliers. Include name, location, and the general range of other stone products available at this source.

GENERAL

Throughout history, humans have relied heavily on wood. We have employed this versatile material for fuel, in tool-making, and especially as a construction material. The long-standing craftsmanship associated with carpentry is on a par with masonry as a highly developed human skill. We build the overwhelming majority of our homes with wood and we furnish them with wood artifacts. It follows that wood has found its way into the built environment as well. We build arbors, pergolas, fences, decks, play equipment, seating, and a wide variety of other site furnishings of wood. In fact, we value wood and its unique properties so much that the depletion of this natural resource has become a serious environmental issue. Virgin or old-growth forests are scarce and endangered resources, with most building lumber coming from carefully managed timber sources.

Shin Residence   Credit: Sundown Gardens

Figure 8-1 This wood arbor and lattice, which provide shade and privacy, shows a high level of craftsmanship in its carpentry.

Figure 8-2 A well-crafted wood fence whose base hints at wainscoting. Its detailing suggests that it surrounds the property of a Colonial-period residence.

Figure 8-3 The intricate detailing of this wood fence elevates its role as a focal point in this landscape.

Wood used in landscape applications carries a unique set of properties and requirements. It is constantly exposed to the elements, so it must have the capacity to stand up to the harmful effects of rain, snow, ice, wind, and exposure to ultraviolet light. Termites, carpenter ants, powder-post beetles, carpenter bees, and other insects are attracted to exposed wood construction for food and shelter. Designers must keep in mind that Mother Nature incessantly strives to reclaim dead wood through a natural cycle of decay and rot, a process that is instrumental for healthy forests to replenish the soils in which new trees and other vegetation can take root and thrive. We must take all diligent measures to delay the inevitable as long as possible, but nature will eventually win out.

Unlike fine interior carpentry and millwork, which often favor hardwoods such as oak, maple, and cherry to create substantial and lasting objects, softwoods are more commonly employed in landscape applications. Pine, fir, and spruce are the most popular and affordable genera of wood used in exterior environments. Cedar, teak, and redwood (from managed sources) are somewhat costlier, but have superior rot and insect resistance. Each is easier to work with, more widely available, grows faster, and costs less than its hardwood cousins. The favored type of wood for landscape construction varies regionally based on tradition and availability.

CHARACTERISTICS OF WOOD

Structurally, wood is the opposite of brittle masonry materials. It is excellent in spanning situations and

Figure 8-4 Overhead arbors create a play of shadow and light.

maintains a great deal of flexibility under stress. Annular growth rings found in trees impart a visible grain to lumber that varies by species. The general strength and stability of a particular species of wood is related to the rate of growth of the tree it comes from. Oaks and beeches tend to grow slowly and

Figure 8-5 A wood boardwalk creates a relaxed and comfortable place to stroll along the waterfront.

develop a tight, stable cell structure and grain that are prized by carpenters and woodworkers. Pines grow faster and yield a lighter wood that is somewhat less stable than oak. Newly harvested wood contains considerable internal moisture and must be dried, by either air-drying (AD) or kiln-drying (KD), before it is suitable for use as a building material. Unmanaged or uneven drying may lead to distortion of the milled lumber.

Because water is a key element in the natural cycle of rot and decay of fallen trees, it is important to minimize any contact with moisture in wood landscape construction. Even rot-resistant species will have a longer life cycle if their exposure to water is minimized. Good surface and subsurface drainage is one significant way in which a landscape designer can reduce the potential for water to damage wood. Another method is the appropriate use of fasteners and brackets that are specifically designed to elevate wood posts above finished grade or anywhere standing water is likely, without sacrificing structural integrity.

Unlike quarried stone or the clay used in the manufacture of bricks, wood is a harvested renewable resource. Its enormous popularity in the landscape,

Figure 8-6 This wood deck functions much like a pier or dock, allowing convenient access to the water while using a minimum of structural components.

especially for residential decking and play equipment, has played a role in increasing the strain on wood resources. Environmentalists and the wood products industry are often at odds over the management of wood resources and practices related thereto.

Landscape designers can play a key role in ensuring that proper forest practices are employed by specifying that lumber must come from a managed source.

COMMON WOOD SPECIES IN LANDSCAPE CONSTRUCTION

As discussed earlier in this chapter, the types of wood used in landscape construction are typically rapid-growing softwoods coming from coniferous species. The popularity and availability of these species vary by region. The most typical species of wood available today are southern yellow pine, sometimes called southern pine, Douglas fir, western red cedar, ponderosa pine, and redwood.

Southern Yellow Pine

Southern yellow pine is native to the southeastern United States, ranging from Texas to the Atlantic coast. *Pinus palustris* may also be known locally as longleaf pine or pitch pine. Southern yellow pine is both economical and extremely versatile as landscape construction lumber. It features relatively high strength compared to other commercial softwoods and offers the advantage of being able to hold fasteners better than many softwoods, making it an ideal choice for decks and play equipment.

Southern yellow pine lacks the natural resistance to insects and rot found in cedar, redwood, and teak, so pressure-treating is strongly recommended for exterior use. Further, it is not particularly admired for its patina. Although beauty is in the eye of the beholder, few would rate the splotchy, aged appearance of unfinished southern yellow pine high on their list of attractive exterior finishes. Painting or staining is strongly recommended.

Douglas Fir

As its genus reveals, the Douglas fir (*Pseudotsuga menziesii*) is not actually a member of the fir (*genus Abies*) family at all. The literal translation of the genus *Pseudotsuga* is "false hemlock." Douglas fir is currently North America's most plentiful softwood species, having surpassed the southern yellow pine to constitute about 20 percent of the continent's total softwood supply. Its native range spans the Rocky Mountains and the Pacific coastal area. In addition to being valued for lumber, Douglas fir is widely used as an evergreen landscape plant.

As a construction material, Douglas fir is very stable and is valued for its strength-to-weight ratio. Its high relative density yields good nail and plate-holding qualities. Its tight cell structure actually poses a challenge during the process of pressure-treating; small incisions must be made in its surface to facilitate chemical penetration. Pressure-treated Douglas fir is an extremely durable wood in exterior applications.

As timber, Douglas fir is sometimes combined with western hemlock and is marketed as "Hem-Fir." Similarly, it may be teamed with western larch and sold commercially as a mix of the two species.

Western Red Cedar

Western red cedar (*Juniperus scopulorum*) is native to the Rocky Mountains, ranging from California to British Columbia. Like Douglas fir, western red cedar is prized for its landscaping value. As a construction material in landscape situations, it is valued for its physical appearance and for its natural preservative, which resists insects and rot. This same preservative will have a corrosive effect on untreated metal fasteners, which can result in discoloration and staining of the wood surface.

Western red cedar has a low relative density compared to other softwoods, making it lighter (21 pounds per cubic foot compared with 34 pcf for southern yellow pine) and thus less costly to transport and easier to manipulate on the construction site. Although cedar contains a natural preservative, it is advisable to apply a protective finish such as stain or paint to increase its service life.

Ponderosa Pine

Pinus ponderosa is another West Coast timber product, with most lumber coming from managed resources in California and Oregon. The popularity of treated ponderosa pine for exterior projects is increasing. Its many applications include exterior decks, planters, arbors, play structures, fences, benches, and storage sheds.

Figure 8-7 *The cedar components of this park shelter benefit from a natural resistance to insects and decay.*

Ponderosa pine is well suited to pressure-treating because chemical preservatives penetrate its sapwood cells deeply and uniformly. It can be treated for above-ground or in-ground contact, and its treated surface is very receptive to paint or stain.

Redwood

Timber milled from the coastal redwood *(Sequoia sempervirens)* has long been prized for its unique beauty and its natural ability to resist insects and rot. Decks, play structures, fences, gazebos, and arbors constructed of redwood make a dramatic statement in a designed landscape. However, as environmental awareness grew in the second half of the twentieth century, a very legitimate concern for the future of California's old-growth redwood forests led to a decline in demand for this wood.

Today, 95 percent of California's old-growth redwood stands are protected and California's rigid Forest Practices Act has resulted in the sustainable management of redwood resources. According to the California Redwood Association, redwoods are the fastest-growing softwood tree species in North America. A tree's rate of growth is a significant factor in successful management of timber resources and in the ability of the species to absorb greenhouse gases. Certification of California redwood by a third party such as the Forestry Stewardship Council or the Sustainable Forest Initiative assures landscape designers that they are making a sustainable choice when selecting redwood for their project.

Teak

At the upper end of the price scale, teak's primary use in the landscape is in the construction of outdoor furniture. Teak *(Tectona grandis)* performs admirably in the elements and ages to a beautiful silvery-gray patina. Unlike the species discussed earlier, teak is considered a hardwood rather than a softwood. As a testament to its exterior durability, teak is also used for ship decking.

Teak is not native to North America. It grows in such tropical climates as India, Indonesia, Burma, Malaysia, and Central America. The demand for teak has resulted in significant deforestation in locations where forest management practices are lax, and unscrupulous trade practices have been marked by more than widespread environmental degradation. Military interventions associated with the teak trade, along with violations of both human and animal rights, have been documented in less well-regulated regions. In the first decade of the twenty-first century, this situation remains in flux.

Considering its questionable social and environmental history, designers need to be diligent in choosing teak elements grown in managed, reforested locations.

WOOD STANDARDS

Sizing

Lumber is milled in standardized dimensions, but the relative ease with which it can be cut allows it to be cut or ripped into any dimension a designer requires. The specified dimensions of lumber are *nominal,* that is, in name only. Prior to sale, lumber is dried and surfaced. *Surfacing* refers to the finish planing of wood in which some of its surface is removed. Because of this surfacing, and to a lesser extent because of drying, the actual dimensions of lumber are smaller than the nominal dimensions. The familiar *two-by-four* actually has a cross-section that measures 1½ by 3½ inches. This reduction of half an inch is the typical difference between the actual and nominal dimensions of the edges and faces of dimensional lumber. Understanding and working with nominal dimensions is critically important for designers when they detail jointery and configure precise connections between various wood members.

Grading

The uniform grading of softwood lumber is another important aspect of successful work with wood in landscape applications. The stamp applied to lumber reveals a number of key characteristics. It indicates what kind of tree the lumber came from, its relative quality, and the amount of moisture that was present in the wood when it was surfaced. The stamp also identifies where the lumber was milled and which agency performed the grading. For designers, quality (also called *grade*) and species are the most relevant designations of lumber.

Pressure-Treating

Many species of softwoods lack any natural resistance to insects and rot and must be chemically treated to survive in the harsh exterior environment. Pressure-treating is a method of preserving wood by subjecting it to a chemical bath under high pressure, which forces the protective solution into the cells of the wood. The element copper is toxic to insects and decay-causing fungi. Until 2003, chromated copper arsenate (CCA) was the chemical most commonly used in this process. Unfortunately, CCA was found to pose serious health hazards, particularly to carpenters who were frequently exposed to CCA-bearing sawdust; this prompted the Environmental Protection Agency to restrict the use of pressure-treated wood in residential installations. Currently, the most widely used alternative to CCA is alkaline copper quat (ACQ).

Wood Finishes

Designers may opt to finish wood to achieve both visual and protective benefits. Finishes offer the choice of color and richness, and may alter the way the patina of a particular species develops over time. Pressure-treating may offer effective protection against rot and decay, but it weathers to an unwelcome splotchy gray in a relatively short time. Wood finishes can enhance the visual appearance of exterior softwoods while providing another level of defense against the elements, extending the life of the wood. Wood finishes can be

divided into two broad categories: those that sit on the surface of the wood, forming a membrane to keep the elements out; and those that penetrate into the wood beneath the surface, enhancing its overall water repellency.

Painting wood is an effective way to achieve a precise color to complement an architectural or natural context. Modern latex paint can endure in the exterior environment and is available in a limitless spectrum of hues. However, paint sits on the surface of wood and will not stand up to the heavy foot traffic inherent in use as deck surfaces and treads. Painted wood will effectively resist water penetration and the effects of ultraviolet light, but works best in combination with a paintable water repellent. To remain effective in its role as a water repellent, painted wood requires vigilant maintenance. Any location where paint has peeled or has been worn away is essentially bare wood, susceptible to the impacts of water and insects.

Wood stains that penetrate into the surface of the wood are more durable in traffic areas because they reside on and beneath the plane of traffic. They extend the life of wood by making its surface impervious to water. Pigmentation can be added to stain to impart a tone or color to the wood. Unlike paint, which completely conceals the wood beneath a membrane, semitransparent stains allow the natural grain of the wood to play a role in its overall visual appearance.

ENVIRONMENTAL CONSIDERATIONS OF WOOD

Environmentalists and the wood-products industry have clashed over timber practices for decades. According to Will Raap, a champion of sustainable landscape practices, "The earth's forests are its lungs; they produce oxygen, which is vital for sustaining all life. Equally important, forests absorb carbon dioxide from the atmosphere and retain it in their trunks and limbs and roots" (Raap, undated Web article).

This process of absorbing and retaining carbon dioxide is called *carbon sequestration*. The deforestation of old-growth forests is accompanied by widespread environmental impacts, including loss of wildlife habitat, reduction of groundwater infiltration and quality, loss of carbon-scrubbing foliage, reduction of biodiversity, increased erosion of topsoil, and increased sedimentation of waterways, among a very long list of deleterious effects. A strong demand for wood products, coupled with a growing recognition of the damage incurred by unmanaged clear-cutting, has led to increasingly stringent regulation of forest resources. It is important that designers specify that any wood used in their projects must come from well-managed sources and be certified by third-party review.

Sustainable Forest Initiative

The Sustainable Forest Initiative (SFI) was established in the mid-1990s by the American Forest & Paper Association (AF&PA), with the primary mission of developing a code of responsible environmental behavior for sustainable forestry management. The SFI serves as a certification program, assuring builders, designers, and consumers that forests are managed using sustainable practices. Today, the SFI is a fully independent third-party certifying organization.

Forest Stewardship Council

Quoting from its charter, "the Forest Stewardship Council (FSC) is a nonprofit organization devoted to encouraging the responsible management of the world's forests. FSC sets high standards that ensure forestry is practiced in an environmentally responsible, socially beneficial, and economically viable way." Like the Sustainable Forest Initiative, the Forest Stewardship Council serves to assess and certify that wood and paper products are grown and harvested using sustainable practices.

SYNTHETIC WOOD

Designers are often prone to eschew as unworthy any material that hints at artifice. It is often true that synthetic materials lack a sense of genuineness or authenticity. This attitude may be appropriate much of the time, but designers must also be receptive to new products that offer clear advantages in terms of cost, durability, and environmental performance. Synthetic, or *composite,* wood is such a material. Synthetic wood does not require sealing, staining, or finishing; needs little maintenance; has superior stability; and lasts

significantly longer than real wood. Those features alone make it worthy of our attention. Adding to its appeal, synthetic wood may also contain recycled plastic and wood-waste byproducts, and its use reduces the pressure for natural wood resources.

The most common use of synthetic wood is in decking. Outdoor decks are enormously popular and generate a significant demand for exterior wood. However, exposure to weather and traffic results in a relatively high level of maintenance if one is to preserve a safe and attractive deck. Synthetic wood has superior water resistance and its surface stands up well to foot traffic.

Synthetic decking is available under a variety of brand names, and not all products are identical in composition. Generally speaking, though, synthetic decking is a composite of wood-industry byproducts or recycled products (including wood fibers and sawdust), combined with some form of plastic, such as polyethylene or PVC, which may also be recycled. This mix of wood and plastic gives synthetic wood its excellent resistance to rot and insects, and resistance to the cracking, splitting, and weathering common to natural wood decks. Manufacturers offer excellent warranties on composite wood, far exceeding those available on natural wood.

The major criticism of synthetic wood products invariably falls into the visual appeal category. Manufacturers are attempting to address these concerns with increasingly realistic colors and textures, but a more daunting challenge lies in the lack of an attractive patina with age. The wood component of the blend does yield some protection against fading due to ultraviolet light, but certain hues (such as deep reds) tend to fade more than others. Also, although synthetic decking may be cost-effective over its life cycle, the initial installation cost may be significantly higher than with more economical woods, such as pressure-treated southern yellow pine. The first generation of composite wood products were specifically targeted as a substitute for decking, with the posts, beams, joists, and rails still made from natural wood. More recently, synthetic wood products are finding their way into some other high-maintenance components, such as posts and railings, as well as exterior fencing.

PHOTO GALLERY

Wood performs admirably in the designed landscape. This portfolio of wood landscape elements demonstrates its beauty, functionality, and tremendous versatility.

Figure 8-8 Wood seating and a wood arbor contrast with the surrounding glass, stone, and steel skyscrapers to create a setting for casual relaxation in this urban park.

Figure 8-9 *Wood architecture as a landscape element. This gazebo provides a destination and a focal point along the garden path.*

Figure 8-10 *This commercial-grade deck extends the usable outdoor space of the architecture. Its roof permits use in all types of weather.*

Figure 8-11 A rustic, rough-hewn rail fence set behind a granite block curb establishes a casual theme at the entrance to this neighborhood park.

Figure 8-12 Rustic, unfinished wood pickets create a transparent yet effective barrier, especially when combined with the visual mass of a stone retaining wall.

Figure 8-13 This simple yet inviting bench is set back from the main traffic pattern, and provides a masonry "impact area" to keep feet dry.

Figure 8-14 A unique wood bench that takes on the appearance of sculpture without sacrificing function or human comfort.

LEARNING ACTIVITIES

1. Locate a Website for a municipal building department of your choice.
   a. Identify the specific requirements for a building permit for a residential deck, including the cost of the permit and the required documentation.
   b. Identify any guidelines, documents, or technical assistance the municipality provides for deck design and construction.

2. Visit a builder's supply or home improvement store.
   a. Locate the construction lumber and identify the species and finish available.
   b. Locate and identify any synthetic wood products available.

CHAPTER 9 MATERIALS IN COMBINATIONS

GENERAL

When young designers are first presented with the myriad of choices of hardscape materials at their disposal, the result is sometimes a dizzying buffet of materials, colors, and finishes. The critique is invariably the same: *"Too busy!"* Yet, multiple materials can coexist wonderfully in the built landscape. Despite contrasting visual characteristics, materials can gain harmony and unity by sharing less tangible qualities such as character, richness, patina, and origin. This is a much more subtle form of harmony than the type displayed by several pieces of matched luggage. Brick, granite, and even concrete share a geologic reference in which each speaks of their earthly origins and an ongoing process of change over time. The Japanese design philosophy known as "Wabi-sabi" venerates the notion of age, patina, and even decay in materials.

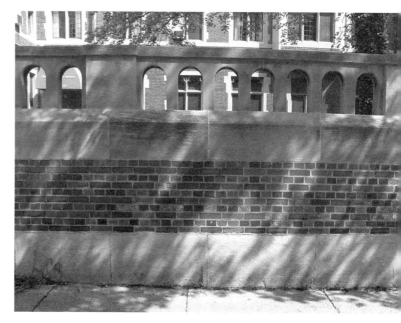

Figure 9-1 A beautifully blended combination of limestone and brick.

Figure 9-2 Brick, granite, and asphalt block unit pavers. These pavements work in harmony despite their differences in color, texture, and geometry.

Figure 9-3 Steps and pavement composed of granite, brick, and asphalt block unit pavers. The dramatic juxtaposition of materials in this installation appears unexpected and even whimsical.

Figure 9-4 The travertine and brick in this Italian piazza have acquired a rich patina from age, weathering, and traffic.

Figure 9-5 The dramatic contrast of these large granite unit pavers set against the fine texture of brick forms a dramatic and memorable node in this Boston urban space.

Figure 9-6 Honed granite, cobblestones, and brick pavers combine to lend a dignified and historic feel to this public garden space. The radial and concentric arrangement of each material, including the stone curbing and the seating, work in concert to unify this space.

Figure 9-7 A playful intersection of asphalt block unit pavers, brick, honed stone steps, and split-face granite walls. Even the offset arrangement of the metal handrail reinforces the lines of the pavement.

Figure 9-8 The paving, walls, and copings in this church courtyard mix three contrasting types of stone set in close proximity.

Figure 9-9 Granite and brick skillfully arranged into a paving medallion with a unique bronze drain cover in the center. Note the radial soldier course of bricks surrounding the granite and the radial rowlock arrangement of the bricks in the center. Details such as these suggest a masterful and sophisticated hand at work.

Figure 9-10 This simple memorial garden combines precast pavers, limestone details, and exposed aggregate concrete paving to suggest repose and dignity.

Previous chapters presented materials and their characteristics individually. This chapter celebrates materials in ensembles of two, three, and more, where their artful combinations represent something much greater than the sum of their individual qualities. Skillful designers can deftly combine multiple materials without compromising the cohesiveness of the overall design. Each of these images presents materials in successful combinations. As an exercise, count and identify the various landscape materials presented in each image, then try to envision the number of construction details that were necessary to bring these spaces to reality.

GENERAL

The built environment is by far the best laboratory for studying and evaluating the success or failure of landscape details. Successful landscape designers need to develop two visions. One is the broad vision of the big picture; the broad swath of the built landscape. The other is the more microscopic vision of the details all around us, underfoot, everywhere. This student learning activity, entitled a *Photographic Journal of Landscape Details,* maintains the desired outcomes of getting students to look, to analyze, and to hypothesize about why details either work or do not work.

Specific Requirements

During the course of the academic semester, each student is to develop a photographic journal of no fewer than forty landscape details. Twenty photographs are to feature details that the student considers successful in terms of their aesthetics, function, and/or durability. Another twenty photographs should highlight details that have clearly failed in some fashion.

Each photograph will be accompanied by the following written information:

- General description. *Examples:* Cast-in-place concrete sidewalk; cobblestone plaza.
- General location. *Examples:* The sidewalk on the 200 block of Main Street; the courtyard behind the English Building.
- For the twenty successful details, the student is to compose a brief paragraph indicating why he or she finds merit in the detail.
- For the twenty unsuccessful details, the student is to compose a similar paragraph that identifies the

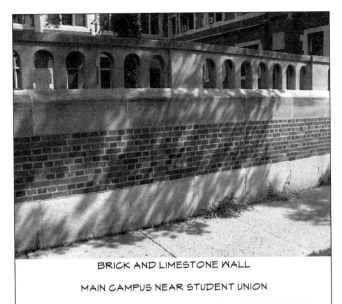

BRICK AND LIMESTONE WALL

MAIN CAMPUS NEAR STUDENT UNION

BRICK AND LIMESTONE COMPLEMENT ONE ANOTHER
AND THE ADJACENT ARCHITECTURE.
BOTH MATERIALS HAVE ACQUIRED AN APPEALING
PATINA.

Example of a journal entry for a successful landscape detail

BRICK-IN-MOARTAR PAVING BAND SET IN
CONCRETE SIDEWALK.

DOWNTOWN, ACROSS FROM THE COURTHOUSE.

BRICKS ARE FRACTURED AND SPALLING
AND THE MORTAR JOINTS ARE FAILING.

THERE IS NO VISIBILE EVIDENCE OF
EXPANSION MATERIAL IN THIS DETAIL

Example of a journal entry for an unsuccessful landscape detail

specific failure (cracking, displacement, spalling, etc.) and contains the student's speculation about the cause of the failure (exposure to standing water, excessive loading, lack of expansion joints, etc.). Special note should be made of any failure that has resulted in a dangerous or hazardous situation.

All photographs are to be original, taken exclusively by the student. No photographs are to be downloaded from the Web nor shared among students.

In the interest of environmental sustainability, students are encouraged to submit their photographic journals using digital media, such as PowerPoint®, Movie Maker®, or other widely available presentation software that is compatible with the instructor's technical capabilities.

Landscape details are everywhere, but academic field trips to noteworthy landscapes represent unique opportunities to photograph and catalog a wide variety of landscape details. Students of landscape design should develop the habit of bringing a camera and sketchbook along wherever they go, and of capturing details for their libraries. An ever-expanding catalog of details, successful or otherwise, will ultimately enhance a designer's repertoire significantly, broadening his or her perception of the possibilities while avoiding the pitfalls associated with designing the built landscape.

BIBLIOGRAPHY

Beall, Christine. *Masonry: Concrete Brick Stone*. Upper Saddle River, N.J.: Creative Homeowner, 1998.

California Redwood Association. *Redwood: The Natural Choice for Green Building*. Bulletin, 2007.

Campbell, James W. P., and Will Pryce. *Brick: A World History*. London: Thames & Hudson Ltd., 2003.

Ferguson, Bruce K. *Porous Pavements: Integrative Studies in Water Management and Land Development*. Boca Raton, Fla.: CRC Press, 2005.

Hayward, Gordon. *Stone in the Garden: Inspiring Designs and Practical Projects*. New York: W. W. Norton, 2001.

Hopper, Leonard J. *Landscape Architectural Graphic Standards*. New York: John Wiley & Sons, 2007.

Indiana Limestone Institute of America, Inc. *Indiana Limestone Handbook*, 18th ed. Bedford, Indiana: Author. 1972

Kirkwood, Niall. *The Art of Landscape Detail: Fundamentals, Practices, and Case Studies*. New York: John Wiley & Sons, 1999.

Marks, Howard. "Asphalt: The Environmentally Sustainable Pavement." *Hot Mix Asphalt Technology 12*, no. 1 (January–February 2007): 3–6.

National Asphalt Pavement Association. *Porous Asphalt Pavements*. Information Series 131. Washington, D.C.: Author, 2003.

———. *Recycling Practices for HMA*. Special Report 187. Washington, D.C.: Author, 2000.

Raap, Will. *Finally, Eco-Smart Teak Furniture from the Americas!* The Founder's Corner, undated Web article.

Rollings, Raymond S., and Marian P. Rollings. *Design Considerations for the UNI Eco-Stone Concrete Paver*. Palm Beach Gardens, Fla.: UNI-Group, 1999.

Samuelson, Lisa J., and Michael E. Hogan. *Forest Trees: A Guide to the Eastern United States*. Upper Saddle River, NJ: Pearson Education, 2006.

"A Solar Reflectance Index Primer." *Interlocking Concrete Pavement Magazine* 14, no. 4 (November 2007): 26–28.

Sovinski, Rob W. *Brick in the Landscape: A Practical Guide to Specification and Design*. New York: John Wiley & Sons, 1999.

Thompson, William J., and Kim Sorvig. *Sustainable Landscape Construction: A Guide to Green Building Outdoors*. Washington, D.C.: Island Press, 2000.

Weinberg, Scott S., and Gregg A. Coyle, eds. *Materials for Landscape Construction*, vol. 4. Washington, D.C.: Landscape Architecture Foundation, 1992.

Winterbottom, Daniel M. *Wood in the Landscape: A Practical Guide to Specification and Design*. New York: John Wiley & Sons, 2000.

INDEX

Aggregate:
   base course, 16
   dense-graded, 19
   exposed, 6
   grading of, 7, 11
   in concrete, 77
Air bush, 75
Alloys, 92, 95, 99–100
Aluminum, 92–93, 98–99
   shaping of, 99
American Concrete Institute, 77
American Forest & Paper Association, 145
Americans with Disabilities Act, 9, 19
Aspdin, Joseph, 58
Asphalt Institute, 14–15
Asphalt:
   color coating of, 18
   decorative, 16
   full-depth, 15
   hot-mix, 14–17, 21, 80
   imprinted, 16
   porous,18–19
   setting bed, 22
   thermal fusing of, 17
   unit pavers, 21, 22
   warm-mix, 20
Authenticity, 117

Basalt, 114–115
Bitumens, 14–15
Bituminous concrete, 13.
     See also Asphalt
Bluestone, 121–122
Bolts, 104–106
   carriage head, 105
   countersinking, 105
   hex head, 105
   lag bolt, 106
   square head, 105
Bond-breaker, 107
Brass, 92–93
Brick Industry Association 29, 54
   Technical Notes, 54
   Brick in Architecture, 54